Artists Handbooks
Money Matters
the artist's financial guide

edited by
**Sarah Deeks,
Richard Murphy &
Sally Nolan**

with additional material by
Sharon McKee & Debbie Duffin

an
PUBLICATIONS

AN Publications

By giving access to information, advice and debate, AN Publications aims to:

- empower artists individually and collectively to strengthen their professional position
- raise awareness of the diversity of visual arts practice and encourage an equality of opportunity
- stimulate good working practices throughout the visual arts.

The Authors Are partners in Murphy, Deeks, Nolan, Chartered Accountants, Gardner House, Broomhill Road, London SW18 4JQ. They specialise in working with artists, craftspeople and photographers.

Series editor David Butler

Reader Val Murray

Sub-edit & Index Heather Cawte Winskell & Debra Webb (100 Proof)

Cover image Photograph by Moira Conway

Design & layout Neil Southern

Grant aid Arts Council of England

Printer Mayfair Printers, Print House, Commercial Road, Sunderland SR2 8NP

ISBN 0 907730 26 4

AN Publications is an imprint of Artic Producers Publishing Co Ltd
PO Box 23, Sunderland SR4 6DG, tel 0191 567 3589

Contents

Contents

About this book

How many times have you asked, *'Is my telephone bill tax-deductible?';* *'Should the local authority be deducting tax from me when I am self-employed?'; 'How do I fill in my tax return?'* And how many times have you felt, *'I don't want to be spending my time finding this out when I could be in the studio. I just want answers.'*

Money Matters answers these questions. Written by Sarah Deeks, Richard Murphy and Sally Nolan, partners in Murphy Deeks Nolan, Chartered Accountants, (which deals with a large number of artists, craftspeople and photographers), *Money Matters* reflects advice provided over time to real artists. It is essentially of a practical nature with advice that is appropriate to your needs on keeping records, managing finances and surviving the pitfalls of self-employment. *Money Matters* addresses visual artists but the advice is equally appropriate to film-makers, musicians, actors, writers, etc.

Money Matters is designed so you can read it from beginning to end or ask it specific questions. It is indexed, cross-referenced, and, will lead you to other information sources. It is a book to be used. And it is a single source of professional advice so you don't have to waste your time running after information.

The actual keeping of accounts is dealt with at the end of the book. There are two chapters on book-keeping. If you are not VAT-registered, look at the first; if you are VAT-registered, look at the second. How do you know whether you need to be VAT-registered? Look at the chapter 'VAT and the Artist'. Ask *Money Matters* questions and you will get answers.

The tax system for all individuals and partnerships is currently undergoing a major change. This means that new businesses created after 6 April 1994 are taxed in a different way to those created before that date but eventually everyone will be will operate under the same system and the book is written for all self-employed artists. For the sake of simplicity *Money Matters* does not consider the old rules. Established artists should read the section on the transition rules from the old system to the new system.

1 • Turning professional

Hobby or self-employment

In order to qualify as self-employed, the art work you do does not have to be on a full-time basis. It is important to seek advice if you are unsure whether your work is what the Inland Revenue defines as a hobby business or proper self-employment. There is a very thin dividing line between art as a hobby and as a trade or business.

Sometimes if you are only undertaking a low level of work you may not have to pay any tax depending on your personal tax position. see page 13 But if the Inland Revenue finds out you are regularly selling work and you are not registered as self-employed, they are likely to take a much stricter view of your affairs and ask a lot of questions.

There are no hard and fast rules for determining what is a hobby business and what is a self-employment, but there are several things you should bear in mind. A person undertaking a hobby business does not do it with a particular view to making a profit. If you paint, for example, in your spare time, occasionally exhibit locally and are lucky to sell a piece of work, then provided the amount is not too significant, ie not more than a few hundred pounds, you will not normally be considered as self-employed.

Another indicator of whether or not a business is a hobby or self-employment is whether it is your main source of income. If it is, there is a much higher risk that the Inland Revenue can argue that you are trading. The Inland Revenue could also take consideration of the amount of time that you spend on the work. If you have a separate studio, even at home, and you do spend a great deal of time on your work and sell some of it, then you could be considered to be trading.

Finally, if you hold yourself out as being an artist rather than see page 11 just having art as a hobby, and you are actively selling work, then you probably are self-employed.

The main things to bear in mind are whether you are actually selling your work and how an independent person would view the work that you do. If in doubt ask for advice or register as a self-employed person.

Trading status

There are five main types of trading status:

* Being a **sole trader** and working on your own as the owner or proprietor of the business.
* Incorporating a **limited company** and becoming a director and shareholder of it.
* Being a **partnership**, ie two or more artists joining up and working under a common name and sharing all income and costs.
* Becoming a **cooperative**, working mostly as an incorporated business but with a high level of management participation by all those working in the studio.
* Working in a **joint venture**, two sole traders working under a common name but running their accounts and businesses entirely separately.

When choosing a trading status several points need to be taken into consideration. The main choice however is whether to be a limited company or not. The advantages of being a limited company lie in the answers you would give to the following questions. If you can answer 'yes' to any of these questions then you could consider being a limited company.

* Will you be working on short production runs, or even going into manufacture?
* Is there a great deal of risk to the work that you do? Are you likely to be sued for any reason?
* Do you always owe a lot of money to creditors, your bank, Customs & Excise or the Inland Revenue? Note that in practice, even if you are a limited company, banks may require a personal guarantee against default on all significant loans and overdrafts, and the Inland Revenue can ask you personally for tax and National Insurance on your director's salary.
* Would your business be seriously damaged by a large bad debt?
* Would your image be enhanced by being a limited company?
* Do you require outside investors to put money into your business?

If you are not working with other people then the liklehood is you will be a sole trader. But if you think there is a chance you should form a limited company, talk with your accountant or professional advisor, since the potential costs of making the wrong decision are high. It is very difficult to get rid of a limited company once it has been incorporated, whereas turning into a limited company a sole tradership or partnership is usually fairly easy after they have been trading for a while, as long as you have not made significant losses.

A limited company can be incorporated by your accountant or solicitor. If you wish to do this yourself, then contact a company formation agency, advertised in such places as Yellow Pages. If you incorporate a limited company and become a director and shareholder, instead of being able to take money from the business for your own personal expenses you will have to become an employee, with tax and National Insurance deducted from all money you take from the company. In most cases unless you are able to undertake some kind of dividend planning this will add 10.2% by way of employer's National Insurance to your costs.

There are very stringent company law requirements you have to adhere to if you incorporate as a limited company. You have to file an annual return and your accounts in a statutory format with the Registrar of Companies. You also have to have a report on the accounts by a reporting accountant if your sales are more than £90,000 per year and an audit if your sales are more than £350,000 a year. All this will add significantly to your costs and should not be dismissed lightly.

Whilst there can be no hard and fast rules as to trading status, it is notable that most artists are sole traders.

Working with others

If you are going to work with other artists then you need to think about the following points.

Partnerships

Partnerships are separate legal entities from the two or three or more individuals who are partners in them. If you are becoming a partnership it is wise to have an agreement drawn up, stating partnership policies and individual partners' rights and obligations.

Unless you are very confident that you can trust all the other partners absolutely, then this can sometimes be a difficult medium to trade under. The main reason is that partners have joint and several liability to each other, ie if one partner defaults on a partnership debt the others are still liable. However for tax purposes the partnership's profit is divided between the partners in their agreed ratios and each partner is then responsible for tax on their share.

A partnership is not always the ideal medium for an artist to work under because the client usually wants to commission the work of an individual, not the work of an artist under an umbrella group, unless the group has a high reputation.

Joint ventures

If you do feel you need to pool your resources, then having a joint venture can often be better than a partnership. The artists preserve their individuality but choose to act together when it is to their advantage, eg better discounts can be obtained by buying in bulk, a studio or exhibition stand can be shared and mutual support given. This often happens where work is placed with a studio in which a fine artist, an illustrator and a graphic designer, all sole traders, share and work on some projects together, pooling their particular talents and sharing costs, or two textile designers who work in different ways but share trade show stands and public relations costs.

If you are proposing to adopt this route then you must make sure you keep your records completely separate. If one person pays out costs on behalf of the others, they invoice these onto the others correctly. It should be borne in mind that these re-charges should be added into your calculations to see whether you should be registered for VAT. This situation is more complicated than working on your own, and you may need an accountant to agree matters between you. You may also like to have some basic agreements drawn up in case you have any disputes.

If the relationship becomes more permanent and all projects are worked on jointly, it might be better to create a partnership. Customs & Excise can sometimes consider that you are a partnership even if you don't, especially if one participant is VAT-registered and the others are not, or if your joint income is more than the VAT registration limit. In this case all participants should register for VAT, or you should trade as a partnership. In this situation you may need to take professional advice to avoid potentially costly mistakes.

Cooperatives

How the affairs of an artists' cooperative are worked out depends on its constitution and construction. Quite often they are constructed as limited companies and therefore the same formalities apply. If several people are involved, limited company status may be sensible, since the higher costs are shared, and a more formal route often works better where more artists are involved.

Limited companies

It is beyond the scope of this book to discuss in detail the workings of limited companies. There are many detailed and specific rules and you will need professional advice to help you keep on the right side of the law. There are however certain things which are specific to limited companies:

* The limited company is distinct and separate from the directors and shareholders in the company. This means that artists working for a limited company are considered to be employees so tax and National Insurance must be operated on all money taken by them from the company. Such rules apply as much to shareholder/directors as any other person. Note that your National Insurance bills will almost invariably be higher than if you are self-employed.

see **15 • Artist as employee**, pages 90-92

* A limited company of any size has to prepare accounts in accordance with the law in a prescribed format. If the company has sales of less than £90,000, it does not need to have any report by an accountant, although you will probably need professional help to prepare the accounts in accordance with company law. If the company has sales between £90,000 and £350,000 a year, then it will need a report by a reporting accountant. If the company has income above £350,000, it will have to be audited and a registered auditor will need to be appointed. Any company can choose to have an audit. The costs of undertaking this work are usually much higher than for preparing the accounts of a self-employed person and there are strict time limits for completion, which must be within ten months of the accounts' year end, and there are fines for failing to comply.

Companies House:
Registrar of Companies, Companies House, Crown Way, Cardiff CF4 3UZ (England & Wales)

Companies House, 100-102, George Street, Edinburgh EH2 3DJ (Scotland)

Registrar of Companies, 64 Chichester Street, Belfast BT1 4JX (N. Ireland)

* Companies' accounts and an annual return form have to be filed at Companies House once a year. There is an annual filing fee of £18.

* Benefits provided to a director, or an employee earning over £8,500, of a limited company, such as a car, will attract a benefit-in-kind charge which will increase the tax charge on the director or employee. Expenses reimbursed from the company to a director have to be declared to the Inland Revenue each year even if they were spent solely for the company's benefit.

- The directors and shareholders of a company do not have to be the same people, although if you work in your own business which is run as a limited company it is quite likely that you will be a director and a shareholder. A company requires at least one director and a company secretary and a minimum of one shareholder.

- If you make losses in a company such that the company has more liabilities than assets then it could be considered to be trading whilst insolvent. As a director you could be liable personally for any unpaid bills or other liabilities if the company goes into liquidation, if you fail to act quickly to stop the losses, to stop trading or appoint a liquidator. If a company goes into liquidation then the directors are liable for any PAYE and National Insurance not deducted from their salaries. A director or shareholder cannot offset any losses made by the company against their own income to obtain a tax benefit, unlike a self-employed person.

If you are in doubt about the trading status you should adopt, consult an accountant. As a general rule being a sole trader is the simplest and cheapest option and very often the most suitable choice for an artist. Unless otherwise noted we assume this to be your choice for the rest of the book.

Self-employed or employed?

It is important to make sure you are genuinely self-employed and not an employee with regard to your freelance artist work, as there are big differences between the types of expenses you can claim and how the collection of the tax is administered. If you are self-employed you pay your own tax directly to the Inland Revenue. If you are an employee, tax and National Insurance should be deducted from your pay and paid over by your employer.

If you work from home, from your own studio, or share a studio with other freelance artists and do work for a variety of people, then it is highly likely that you are self-employed.

There is a grey area – if you believe you are self-employed but do most of your work in a design studio, in a fairly junior position, directed and controlled by more experienced designers, then the Inland Revenue could argue that you are an employee of the studio. The fact that you are not paid for holidays or sickness does not make you self-employed. Nor does the fact that you have only a short-term contract.

Any contract covering your work must be drawn up carefully, and either the studio or yourself should take professional advice from an accountant or solicitor experienced in self-employed / employed status disputes. The fact that a contract states that you are responsible for your own tax does not make you self-employed. The points that the Inland Revenue look at in deciding this are:

- Does anyone else directly control your work?
- Can you make any more money by the way you organise your work?
- Are you required to provide cover in your absence or get some one else to do the work?
- Where do you do the work and what equipment do you use?
- Have you invested money in your business, eg in a studio, equipment or developing a portfolio?
- Can you work for other people and refuse the work?
- Does the person you are working for see you as integral to their business?

You can have several self-employments and several employments in a tax year. Being self-employed and employed are not mutually exclusive.

The fact that the Inland Revenue allows you to register as a self-employed person does not mean it cannot later say that with regard to the particular work in question, it was not self-employment but an employment. If this happens, the Inland Revenue can deny you tax relief on your expenses. The reason is that if you are an employee you can only obtain tax relief on expenses incurred 'wholly, exclusively and necessarily' for the purposes of your work. It is very difficult to obtain tax relief on any expenses if you are categorised as an employee. If you are in doubt ask an accountant to help you but be aware that disputing your 'status' can be costly.

see 'Expenses' in **15 • Artist as employee**, page 91

2 • Starting to trade

The Inland Revenue

When you start working with a view to a profit, you are legally required to tell the Inland Revenue as soon as you start, and no later than on your tax return due for the tax year in which the income starts, which by concession must currently be submitted by 31 October following 5 April on which that year ends. This applies whether or not you have been sent a Tax Return by the Inland Revenue. Failure to do this could render you liable to interest and penalties.

If you have already had dealings with the Inland Revenue and have a tax office reference, then write to that district with the reference number you have, informing them when you started to be a freelance artist. They will send you a form *41G* which asks for fairly straightforward details such as name, address, date of birth, National Insurance number, the date you started, your recent employment history, etc. This should be completed and returned.

If you do not have an existing Inland Revenue reference then you should look up the Inland Revenue in the telephone directory and pick the tax office (Inspector, not Collector, of Taxes) nearest to where you live if you are working from home, or to your studio if you have one. You should then ring them up and ask if that tax office covers your district. If it does, ask for the form and if it does not, ask them for the details of the district which does. Each district should be able to tell you this.

If you have an accountant you may ask them to inform the Inland Revenue for you. If you do, you will need form *64-8* which will enable your accountant to correspond with the Inland Revenue directly on your behalf. It also means they will receive copies of tax assessments issued to you and the Inland Revenue will direct any queries to them, but they will not receive your tax demands or your tax return.

When you notify the Inland Revenue of your self-employment ask them to send you the explanatory booklet *IR28 Starting in Business* which provides further useful information.

The Department of Social Security

When you become a self-employed artist if you believe you will make a profit in excess of Department of Social Security specified limits (£3,260 in the tax year 1995/6) you are legally obliged to make Class 2 National Insurance contributions, which currently amount to £5.75 per week (1995/6). The rate increases each tax year.

If you think you should make contributions then you should contact the Department of Social Security, Class 2 Group, Longbenton, Newcastle, NE98 1YX. You should request the form *CF11,* and a direct debit mandate form if you want to pay by direct debit. Remember to quote your National Insurance number. The forms are quite straightforward, and if you have any problems with them, contact the DSS at Newcastle. You have a choice as to whether you pay your National Insurance contributions by direct debit or cheque, quarterly in arrears. There are now no other alternatives. The direct debit payments are taken from your bank account monthly and vary as to whether there are four or five weeks in a month. The amount taken is £23.00 or £28.75 per month (1995/6). If you pay by cheque you are sent a quarterly demand of £74.75 (1995/6). If you cease in self-employment you must notify the Department of Social Security in Newcastle and cancel your direct debit at the bank if appropriate.

If you do not think you will make profits of £3,260 (1995/6) in a year then you may apply for an exception from liability. To do this you need to go through all the procedures above, completing the form *CF11,* but instead of completing the direct debit mandate form you need to request an exception form *CF10.* The exception form usually asks you to submit accounts, but if you have just started as self-employed you cannot do this. You should simply complete the form telling the Department of Social Security that you have no belief that you are making a profit in excess of £3,260 (1995/6).

If you are not sure about whether you will exceed the profit limit, you can apply for the exception automatically and then make up the contributions later if you have exceeded the limit.

Once you have started making regular contributions it is much harder for you to qualify for an exception, but it is quite easy for you to obtain one for the first year.

If you are unsure about whether you will qualify for the exception at the end of the year, you should earmark some money to pay the contributions by paying an amount equivalent to the National Insurance contributions into a separate interest-earning bank or building society account. You can ask for an exception and then make up the contributions at the end of the year, or if you pay contributions and have made less than the profit limit, you can claim a refund, but you must do this by 31 December following the end of the tax year.

Once you have been granted exception from liability and issued with a certificate, even if your profits exceed the exception limit £3,260 (1995/6) then the DSS will not ask you to pay the contributions for that period unless you want to, but they would be unlikely to grant any further exception certificates unless you can prove that your profit is below the threshold. Do be aware that if you are exempted from liability then this could reduce the amount of your state retirement pension entitlement and your entitlement to some other DSS benefits, unless you pay any other National Insurance, eg Class 1 contributions as an employee.

If you are self-employed you must apply either to Class 2 National Insurance or for an exception. You must not do nothing. This could lead to you having to pay contributions for no benefit, a loss of benefits or both.

The DSS now normally follow Inland Revenue decisions as to status, ie whether a person is self-employed or not. Therefore if you have been categorised as self-employed by the Inland Revenue you have a liability to pay Class 2 contributions. If the Inland Revenue has ruled that you are an employee, then you have no liability to pay Class 2 contributions, but instead Class 1 contributions should be deducted from your pay.

Customs & Excise

When you first become a freelance artist you need not register for VAT immediately unless you think you will either make sales totalling £46,000 in the next thirty days, or you want to register voluntarily.

If neither of these apply, what you must do to ensure you do not need to register at some future date is to keep a month-by-month total of the amount invoiced to your customers or received by way of cash sales or reimbursed expenses. If, before twelve months have elapsed, the sales on your list exceed £46,000 (after 29 November 1994), you need to register for VAT.

If at the end of the first year your sales have not exceeded £46,000 you should continue with your list and at each month end add up the total amounts of sales invoiced for the last twelve months. When you reach the figure of £46,000 (from 29 November 1994), or are very close to it, you must register for VAT.

When you need to register for VAT you must notify your local Customs & Excise office of the need to be registered within thirty days of exceeding the limit. Penalties for failing to register on time are severe.

To register for VAT you will need to complete the form *VAT 1* if you are a sole trader or a limited company, and forms *VAT 1* and *VAT 2* if you are a partnership. You should look up Customs & Excise in the telephone directory to find the office nearest to your studio address, if you have one, or your home address otherwise, and apply to them for the necessary forms at the first possible opportunity.

The consequences of VAT registration are discussed in chapter 19 • Being VAT-registered.

The various government agencies, including the Inland Revenue, DSS and Customs & Excise now work closely together. This means, for example, that if you tell the Inland Revenue that you are self-employed, then the DSS will be expecting you to register to pay Class 2 contributions. Eventually if they do not hear from you, they will contact you. It is always better to have approached them first, and applications for exemption will be more favourably treated if you do.

Finding an accountant

Whether you will need an accountant depends upon the trading medium you are using, your financial experience, how much financial and accounting work you wish to do yourself, and whether you feel competent to deal with the increasingly complex tax returns and forms issued by the Inland Revenue.

Accounting and tax requirements are becoming increasingly stringent with frequent changes in the law. If you have a limited company you are legally obliged, as a minimum, to have your accounts prepared in a statutory format and may need an accountant's report or an audit, so you will have to have an accountant authorised to carry out the work, normally a Chartered or Certified Accountant.

The Inland Revenue is very reluctant to help a taxpayer claim the expenses and allowances to which they are entitled, and will usually suggest that they see an accountant.

Having a good accountant can pay for itself in terms of making appropriate tax claims and suggesting relevant expenses as well as making sure that you comply with VAT, tax law and other legalities, preparing your accounts, tax computations and tax returns. Getting things wrong or not knowing the law could be expensive in terms of penalties and interest.

Whether or not you want to use your accountant for bookkeeping depends on your personal preference and financial experience and aptitude. If you have a fairly low number of transactions, and are not VAT-registered then your accountant should be quite cost-effective in doing this work for you. If you have a high number of transactions, it may be worth your while employing a separate book keeper to write up your transactions weekly or monthly.

If you can maintain your own books and records this keeps your accounting and bookkeeping costs down, and means you are much more in control of your business – you know who owes you money, how much your costs are, etc. People in this position usually run better and more profitable businesses.

The best way to find an accountant is to ask fellow artists if they can recommend one. Personal recommendation is usually the best route, and it is well worth asking around. You could try asking any association or any grant giving body for a recommendation. Failing that, you could look up accountants either in your local *Yellow Pages* or telephone directory, but this would give you little idea of specialisation. see **22 • Further information**, page 138 You could telephone the Institute of Chartered Accountants in England & Wales, the Institute of Chartered Accountants in Scotland, the Institute of Chartered Accountants in Ireland or the Chartered Institute of Certified Accountants. The enquiry offices of any of the above may be able to put you in touch with somebody local specialising in your field.

When you go along to see an accountant it is a good idea to find out if they are interested in what you do. It is also worthwhile asking what other clients they have and how large they are. If you are an artist on a low income, then using an accountant who deals mainly with large manufacturing companies would not be a good idea. Other points to bear in mind are:

• How many partners are there and will there be cover whilst they are on holiday or away from the office?

- Do they have expensive offices? You will be paying more if their overheads are high.
- Do they have a good relationship with the Inland Revenue? Feel free to ask them.
- What is their attitude to getting accounts prepared: will they prepare your accounts promptly after you give them your books or will they take a long time to do the work?
- Do they seem professional?
- Do you like the person you will be dealing with and feel that you can talk to them easily?
- Can you afford them? Discuss costs and their charging structure so you know what you are letting yourself in for.
- Ask what additional services they provide that can enhance your value for money, eg financial advice with commissions rebated to you, grant advice, etc.

Never feel pressurised into using the first accountant you talk to. If you are not happy with them, continue searching until you are.

3 • Tax and self-employment

How is my tax worked out?

If you make a profit as a self-employed artist and the profit is more than your tax free allowances then you will owe income tax. Your profit is calculated by deducting your tax deductible expenses from your income.

Each year tax payers are allocated personal tax allowances. The level of these depends on whether you are single, married, a single parent etc, and these change each year in the budget.

If you deduct your expenses and your allowances from your income, the figure you are left with is your profit. This is taxed at the rates relevant for the year. In the 1995/6 year these rates are 20% on income up to £3,200, 25% on income between £3,201 and £24,300 and 40% on income above this limit.

What if I don't earn enough to pay tax?

If your profit doesn't exceed your tax free allowances, and if you don't have any other sources of income, then you won't owe any tax (but if you have more than one source of income refer to the chapter on the Inland Revenue).

If you make a loss in your self-employment because your expenses are greater than your income then you won't owe any tax. You may be owed tax refunds depending on how much tax you have paid previously, and what you decide to do with the losses. In this situation you may need professional advice to make the best use of the losses.

On what dates do I pay tax?

Tax on self-employed income is paid in two installments – on 1 January in the tax year, and 1 July after the tax year. So tax for 1995/6 is paid on 1 January 1996 and 1 July 1996. Half of the total amount of tax due is paid on each date.

Aren't these dates changing?

From January 1988, the dates on which the tax payments will be due will change under the self-assessment system. Tax payments will then be due on 31 January and 31 July. Each payment will be half of the tax paid in the previous year. Any extra tax owed, or any refund, will be made the following 31 January, together with the tax due for the next year. Appeals will be permitted against the tax paid on account in certain circumstances.

So, if in the year to 5 April 1998 you paid £500 in tax, then for the year to 5 April 1999 you will be due to pay:

- £250 on 31 January 1999 (half the amount paid for 1998)
- £250 on 31 July 1999 (half the amount paid for 1998)

If your accounts for 1999 show you should have paid £600 in tax then you owe a further £100. You will pay this on 31 January 2000 when you will also have to pay the first installment of tax for that year. This is equal to half the tax due for 1999. You now know this to be £600 in total. So you will be due to pay:

- £400 on 31 January 2000 − £300 (half the tax due for 1999) plus £100 (tax you owed from 1999)
- £300 on 31 July 2000 (half the tax due for 1999)

And so on....

What if I pay too much tax?

If you paid £500 tax for 1999, but only owed £400, then:

- on 31 January 2000 you will owe £200 (half of the tax due for 1999) less £100 (your overpayment in 1999) whaich equals £100
- on 31 July 2000 you will owe a further £200 Half of the tax due for 1999)

And so on....

Tax calculation

If you started your self-employment after 6 April 1994 then your income is taxed under the 'current year basis'. If you started self-employments before 6 April 1994 you are taxed on a 'prior year basis'. Artists taxed on prior year basis will move onto current year basis in the tax year ending 5 April 1998. The year ending 5 April 1997 will be a year of transition.

How does current year work?

Current year basis of taxation means income tax will be charged on the profit you earn in the tax year (ending 5 April), or will be based on the profit in your accounts for the twelve months ending in the tax year.

An artist who starts self-employment on 1 May 1994 will prepare their first set of accounts to 31 March 1995. Each tax year thereafter they are taxed on the following sets of accounts:

Tax Year	Accounts Period	Months Taxed
1994/5	1 May 94 – 31 Mar 95	11 months accounts
1995/6	1 Apr 95 – 31 Mar 96	12 months accounts
1996/7	1 Apr 96 – 31 Mar 97	12 months accounts
1997/8	1 Apr 97 – 31 Mar 98	12 months accounts
1998/9	1 Apr 98 – 31 Mar 99	12 months accounts

What if my accounts year doesn't coincide with the tax year?

A artist who starts self-employment on 1 January 1995 and prepare their first accounts to 31 December 1995, and uses 31 December as their end date for following years, would be taxed on the following sets of accounts:

Tax Year	Accounts Year	Period Taxed	Months Taxed
1994/5	1 Jan 95 – 31 Dec 95	1 Jan 95 – 5 Apr 95	3 months, 5 days
1995/6	1 Jan 95 – 31 Dec 95	1 Jan 95 – 31 Dec 95	12 months accounts
1996/7	1 Jan 96 – 31 Dec 96	1 Jan 96 – 31 Dec 96	12 months accounts
1997/8	1 Jan 97 – 31 Dec 97	1 Jan 97 – 31 Dec 97	12 months accounts
1998/9	1 Jan 98 – 31 Dec 98	1 Jan 98 – 31 Dec 98	12 months accounts

You'll see, in this example, that the period 1 January 95 – 5 April 95 is taxed twice – in the tax year 1994/5 and again in the tax year 1995/6. This period, which has been taxed twice, is known as the 'overlap profit' and is deducted from your final taxable profit when you cease to be self-employed (see chapter 20 • Ceasing to trade). This rule is designed to ensure that over the lifetime of yourself-employment the total profits taxed equal the total profits you have made.

Accounting year end

You can see from the amount of overlap profit in the example above that it's important to choose the year end date of your accounts with care. Choice of year end depends on your personal circumstances, how much you envisage your profits or losses will be, and how long you expect your self-employment to last.

Usually choice of year end is straightforward. The best year end is most likely to be either 31 March or 5 April (for tax purposes 31 March is treated as if it were 5 April). Since this coincides with the tax year there are no overlap profits and you simply pay tax each year on what you earn. It may mean in your first year you have an accounting period shorter or longer than twelve months. For example if you start to be self-employed on 1 November 1995 you would prepare accounts for five months and five days – to 5 April 1996.

But a year end of 5 April may not always be the right choice. For example, if you make a loss in your first year (or a very low profit) but expect profits to rise dramatically in the next year and then stay high, you may obtain a cash flow advantage by choosing an alternative date. Be aware however, if you adopt a year end other than 5 April you will have more tax to pay when you cease self-employment (see chapter 21 • Ceasing to trade). You may need to seek professional advice in this circumstance.

How could not choosing 5 April year end be advantageous?
An artist who starts self-employment on 1 June 1995, whose first accounts to 31 May 1996 show a loss of £5000, and whose accounts to 31 May 1997 and 1998 both show a profit of £20,000, will pay tax on the following profits:

Tax Year	Account Year	Period Taxed	Months Taxed	Profit £
1995/6	1 Jun 95 – 31 May 96	1 Jun 95 – 5 Apr 96	10 months, 5 days	Nil
1996/7	1 Jun 95 – 31 May 96	1 Jun 95 – 31 May 96	12 months	Nil
1997/8	1 Jun 96 – 31 May 97	1 Jun 96 – 31 May 97	12 months	20,000
1998/9	1 Jun 97 – 31 May 98	1 Jun 97 – 31 May 98	12 months	20,000

If, instead of choosing a year end of 31 May, the artist chose a year end of 5 April they would pay tax on the following profits:

Tax Year	Accounts Year	Period Taxed	Months Taxed	Profit £
1995/6	1 Jun 95 – 5 Apr 96	1 Jun 95 – 5 Apr 96	10 months, 5 days	Nil
1996/7	6 Apr 96 – 5 Apr 97	6 Apr 96 – 5 Apr 97	12 months	20,000
1997/8	6 Apr 97 – 5 Apr 98	6 Apr 97 – 5 Apr 98	12 months	20,000

So by choosing the year end of 31 May, as in the first example, tax on £20,000 is deferred for a year. The disadvantage is upon cessation. If the artist ceased self-employment on 5 April 1998, with a 5 April year end the tax would all have been paid year by year. But with a 31 May year end, if the artist ceased self-employment on 31 May 1998 they would still owe tax in 1998/99 on £20,000 of income. Overlap relief is given on cessation but because of the loss in the first period this would be nil.

The price of obtaining an initial cash flow advantage is of far greater uncertainty on cessation. This would be exacerbated if an artist was self-employed for a long-time and was unaware that there would be a tax liability on cessation. Even if there were overlap profits to off-set against tax due on cessation, over time these would be eroded by inflation. Remember the current tax system is designed to ensure that over the life time of your business you pay tax on all your self-employed profits.

Overlap profits

These will occur where a year end of 5 April is not used. It is important to try to avoid too much profit being taxed in both the first and second years and therefore becoming an overlap profit, which can only be off-set upon ceasing in self-employment.

In the example on the previous page, with a year end of 31 May, if the profit in the year ended 31 May 1996 had been £20,000 followed by a loss of £5,000 in the year to 31 May 1997 the profit position on these would have been as follows:

Tax Year	Accounts Year	Period Taxed	Months Taxed	Profit £
1995/6	1 Jun 95 – 31 May 96	1 Jun 95 – 5 Apr 96	10 months, 5 days	16,690
1996/7	1 Jun 95 – 31 May 96	1 Jun 95 – 31 May 96	12 months	20,000
1997/8	1 Jun 96 – 31 May 97	1 Jun 96 – 31 May 97	12 months	Nil

This demonstrates the dangers of a year end other than 5 April where profits fall and the overlap profit of £16,690 would only be available to be off-set against the profits above if the designer ceased to be self-employed. You need to choose a year end other than 5 April with the utmost care.

Changing year ends

The best solution to the above problem would be for the artist to change their year end to 5 April. This means taxable profits in 1996/7, instead of being £20,000, would be £20,000 (profit for 1995/6) less £16,690 (already taxed in 1995/6) – which equals £3310 – plus a proportion of the loss of £5000 equivalent to 10 months, 5 days (approximately £4200). This brings us to 5 April 1997 and gives a taxable profit for that year of £3310-£4200 – ie there is no profit to tax.

How do I change my year end?

There are rules to determine whether or not you can change your year end.

- Changes in the first three years are permitted in any circumstance.

- From year four onwards changes must not result in an accounting period being longer than eighteen months and the Inland Revenue must be notified in writing by 31 January following the tax year in which the change is made.

- In addition there must have been no change of year end in any of the last five tax years or, if there has been a change, the latest change must be for a genuine commercial reason. Obtaining a tax or a tax cash flow advantage is not considered to be a genuine commercial reason.

If you notified the Inland Revenue of an accounting year end date when you filled in the form *41G* but subsequently want to make up accounts to a different date, this is not a problem as the date returned on the form *41G* is not binding. But it is advisable to notify the Inland Revenue as soon as you decide on the new date. A detailed consideration of changes of year end are beyond the scope of this book.

Transitional rules

For artists who were self-employed before 6 April 1994, the change from 'prior year basis' to 'current year basis' will take place in the tax year 1996/7. This is known as the year of transition. The tax year 1997/8 will be the first year when all self-employed people are taxed under the current year basis.

How will this happen?

- If your year end is 5 April, then in 1995/6 you will pay tax based on your accounts to 5 April 1995.

- In 1997/8 you will pay tax on your accounts to 5 April 1998.
- This means that for 1996/7 the profit on which you pay tax is twelve months out of twenty four from the tax years 5 April 1996 and 1997.

So I can earn high profits and not pay tax?

To stop tax payers distorting their accounts by pushing income into the two years making up the transitional year (thereby paying tax on only half the profit) the Inland Revenue have introduced a series of penalties. These mean if the Inland Revenue believe you have distorted your result you will be penalised and be worse off, not better off.

What if my year end doesn't suit current year basis?

If you prepare your accounts to a date other than 5 April then it may pay you under the new current year basis to change your accounts year end to 5 April because your overlap profit will be reduced (see above 'tax calculation' and 'overlap profit'). Deciding when to change your year end, and choosing the new date, can only be calculated on an individual basis and depends on the trend of each person's profit (or loss). You will probably need to seek professional advice. The Inland Revenue have stated that any changes of year end to 5 April made before 5 April 1997 will be agreed with a minimum of enquiry.

The tax return form

Each year shortly after 5 April you will be sent a tax return form. This requires disclosure of all your sources of income – not just from your work as an artist during the tax year but also any other such as teaching, employments, investment income, interest earned on building society or bank accounts and details of any mortgages, pensions and covenants to charities, etc.

The tax return form states it must be submitted to the Inland Revenue within thirty days. Technically this is the due date, and if you have been remiss in not disclosing a major new source of income the Inland Revenue can impose interest and penalties for failure to submit the return by this date.

In practice this date is not binding for most people and the Inland Revenue requires the return to be submitted by 31 October each year. Failure to do this is more likely to render you liable to interest and penalties.

What information do I put on my tax return?

The important thing to bear in mind when completing your tax return is that it must be completely filled in – ie it must show all your sources of income and all your outgoings whether or not tax has already been deducted. If you are uncertain about whether something should be returned on the form include it anyway just to be on the safe side. Or make an estimate – but tell the Inland Revenue that it is an estimate and why and how you have calculated it.

If you are claiming tax relief for such things as pensions, mortgage interest, you will need to supply supporting vouchers to prove you have paid. These can be obtained on request from the pension companies (ask for an *SEPC* or *PPCC*) and banks and building societies (ask for a *MIRAS 5*).

Likewise if you are claiming a tax refund on, for example, tax deducted from teaching income or dividend credits then you need to send in the original form *P60* (certificate of pay and deductions) or dividend vouchers to support this. Copies will not do, so these original documents must be stored very carefully.

To ensure the return is completed accurately it may be worthwhile having a file to put all relevant tax return information into when you receive it. This is particularly true if you have several different building society accounts or if you have any shares.

What if I fill in my tax return wrongly?

The Inland Revenue places great importance on the accuracy of the tax return as an indicator of how accurate you are in dealing with your financial affairs. Inland Revenue investigations have been known for failure to disclose one building society account – even though there was no tax loss to the Inland Revenue. Where large amounts of interest are paid on bank or building society accounts then the Inland Revenue is notified by the bank or building society of this and will check for discrepancies. If the interest earned on a bank or building society account is much higher than expected, the Inland Revenue may ask you where the money came from that gave rise to the interest paid.

Do I always have to fill in a tax return?

Even if the Inland Revenue does not send you a tax return this doesn't mean you don't have to fill one in. If you don't receive one it may be because you have not notified the Inland Revenue that you are a freelance artist, in which case you should do this straightaway, or you may have forgotten to tell them of a change of address. If you have not received one you should speak to your tax office and request one as soon as you realise they have forgotten you.

If you have an accountant they will help you complete the form and advise you which details they require. An accountant will also check for inconsistencies within the information and help you complete the return accurately. They can only complete the form from the information that you give them, so the onus is still on you to keep everything safely so the return can be completed accurately.

Isn't the tax return form changing?

The personal tax system is currently undergoing a series of major changes. This will result in tax payers assessing their own tax liabilities, by 'self-assessment', rather than the Inland Revenue undertaking the job. There will be a new and much more detailed tax return issued for each tax year from the year ended 5 April 1997 onwards. This will need to be submitted by 30 September 1997 if you want the Inland Revenue to work out your tax (but only from the information you have given on the return), or by 31 January 1998 if you calculate your own tax liability. The new system will impose penalities for failure to file a return on time.

Tax deductible expenses

You can have tax relief on expenses as a self-employed artist if you incur them for the purposes of your business. This means that such expenses are deducted from any self-employed income and you are only taxable on the remainder.

It is essential that receipts and invoices are kept for all relevant expenses and that these are written up in your books of account. Estimates and unsupported cash expenses need not be accepted by the Inland Revenue although negotiation on this point is possible. An accountant would almost certainly have to assist such negotiation.

What if I can't separate business and private expenses?

Where expenses have a dual purpose (both a work and private element, eg telephone, motor expenses) you should write the full amount in your books as you go along. At the end of the year you can make a deduction for the private element or adjust your tax computation. If you are VAT registered remember to only claim back the VAT on the business proportion of the expenses.

If you operate through a limited company, for any item with a dual purpose there will be a benefit in kind charge on the director or higher paid employee concerned, and you should consult your accountant. This area of company tax law is complex and well beyond the scope of this book.

What expenses are allowable?
If you have any doubt about whether a particular expense is allowable it is best to ask your accountant or seek advice (eg from another artist or from the Inland Revenue). The following list will provide general guidance but there are grey areas, and these and your personal circumstances should always be taken into account.

Direct costs
These are costs that you incur to directly create your art. They are always allowable for tax purposes if you are a self-employed artist. They could include:

- art materials of all kinds, paints, canvas, papers, pens
- the cost of any materials incorporated into your work, eg clays if you are a ceramicist or fabrics if you work with textiles
- printing
- photographic reproduction and typesetting if you are in design
- computer costs if you use one for your work

see 'PAYE and National Insurance' **16 • Artist as Employer**, pages 93-95

- studio wages for any staff who help you to directly create your work
- sub-contract costs, for example, a textile design which a self-employed textile designer produces and which is incorporated into a mixed media sculpture by another artist
- agent's commission
- gallery commission.

Overhead expenses
These expenses are more subjective than direct costs but are likely to include:

- rent of your studio, or mortgage interest if the studio is owned as a business asset and has a loan secured on it
- if you work from home a proportion of your rent (not mortgage) depending on how much space you use and how much time you work there – usually 25% based on a 35-40 hour working week out of 168 available hours per week
- if you own your home and pay a mortgage claim a small amount say £6-7 per week, for 'use of your home as a studio' (otherwise you could run into problems with capital gains tax if you sell your house)

- studio bills, eg gas, electricity, telephone and fax, insurance, security, repairs
- home bills, if you rent your home and have your studio there claim the same proportion as for your rent. If you own your home then heat and light costs are usually included in the 'use of home' figure
- home telephone, if you work from home. Estimate or keep a log of the proportion of business calls to domestic calls
- postage
- stationery
- photocopies
- office equipment and sundry costs, eg computer discs, calculator, light bulbs, batteries
- travel, train, bus, tube, taxis but not from home to your studio, which cost is specifically not allowed, so you may need to apportion the costs of a weekly travel card if you have one
- foreign travel, eg painting trips, research. These can be difficult to claim unless some tangible income has resulted
- motor expenses, insurance, road fund, repairs, servicing, MOT, parking, petrol and oil, but only a business proportion based on the proportion of business miles driven to total miles driven
- hotels if working away from home, attending galleries, etc
- subsistence if working away from home – but then only modest amounts otherwise it may count as entertaining which is not allowed
- couriers and delivery costs
- advertising
- promotion, publicity and marketing, eg postcards of your work
- photographic costs for your portfolio and reference purposes
- protective clothing, eg kiln goggles, face masks and safety equipment and an allowance to cover cleaning and maintenance of overalls, aprons, etc. Here an estimate may be accepted, eg approximately £10 per month
- canteen and kitchen – a modest amount to cover tea and coffee whilst working, washing up liquid, toilet rolls, etc
- bad debts, ie people who will not pay you. The expense cancels the sale

- legal costs of chasing people who will not pay you, drawing up terms of trade, gallery and agent agreements, gallery and trade disputes and sundry claims
- accountancy and bookkeeping and business financial services
- bank charges and interest on loans to finance working capital and purchases of equipment and lease and hire purchase interest on business equipment and cars
- books, magazines, journals and newspapers used for reference and research or necessary to keep up to date with the art world, eg *Artists Newsletter*
- subscriptions to organisations, professional bodies and unions relevant to your work, eg National Artists Association
- repairs and renewals, eg to furniture, computers
- research costs to get ideas; this is a subjective area and may include: flowers for a painter who paints floral pieces; a trip to an exhibition of an artist engaging in similar work to yours; cinema and film trips for an animator; theatre visits for a set designer; use of TV and video; but you are unlikely to be able to claim more than 50% of research costs except in specific circumstances
- exhibition costs
- hire of equipment
- staff costs (but see the chapter on the artist as an employer)
- make-up and costumes for performing artists (there are specific guidelines for Equity members which are beyond the scope of this book).

Expenses you can never claim
- entertaining clients, suppliers, the media – or anyone at all; you might like to record the expenses but you can never obtain tax relief on them
- clothes, hair or make-up for presentations, exhibitions, meeting clients, gallery openings
- legal costs for obtaining a studio lease
- home to work travel costs
- personal medical expenses
- capital expenditure – for which there are special rules (see below).

Capital expenditure & allowances

Capital expenditure is expenditure on items which you expect to last for more than one year. There is no legal definition of capital expenditure. It includes not only equipment bought during your accounting year but items which you owned prior to becoming a freelance artist and now use in your business.

What is revenue and what is capital expenditure?

This depends in part on the size of your business. If, for example, you make sales of £5000 a year, then capital expenditure would probably be expenditure on items lasting more than one year and costing over £25. If you are making sales of £20,000 a year, then you might treat anything costing under £100 as revenue expenditure to be written off in the year it is purchased – even if it will last for longer. You would then claim capital allowances on anything costing over £100. There are no hard and fast rules. It is recommended that you disclose your chosen policy to the Inland Revenue for approval.

Does the difference between revenue and capital really matter?

The reason why it is so important to distinguish between capital and ordinary day-to-day running costs is because of the way in which you obtain tax relief on the expenditure. On revenue expenditure you will usually obtain a deduction of 100% of the cost in your accounts. For capital expenditure you claim capital allowances. In most cases these amount to 25% of the cost of the item in the first year, and in following years 25% of the remaining balance having deducted previous claims. The capital allowances are deducted from your profit when you work out your tax.

Calculating capital allowances is complicated and there are detailed rules depending on the type of asset involved. If you have an accountant they will deal with this for you. If you do not use an accountant it is important to remember that you must make a formal claim in writing with your tax computation within two years of your accounts year end. If you don't the Inland Revenue is not obliged to give you any tax relief.

What items can I claim capital allowances on?

The following is equipment or assets on which capital allowances may normally be claimed as long as they are used for the business:

- car, motorbike, bike – but business proportion only
- computer, printer and accessories, typewriter

- camera and photographic equipment (sometimes business proportion only)
- drawing board, desk or table, chair or stool
- work lamps
- light box
- equipment and tools specific to your trade, eg loom for a weaver, wheel, kilns, buckets for a ceramicist, etc
- drawing equipment, stock of brushes, etc
- storage, plan chests, filing cabinet, drawers, shelves, etc
- portfolio cases, briefcase, Filofax, electronic organiser
- stock of slides, projector, epidiascope
- TV and video if used in research – but business proportion only (but note for a video/film/media artist these would count as tools specific to your trade)
- stereo or radio if you need music to work – but business proportion only (but note again for some artists these may be tools specific to your trade – so the whole cost can be offset for business use)
- heater other than central heating
- drying racks and heaters to dry fabrics
- answerphone, fax, telephone and security systems
- exhibition equipment, table, stands and display items, frames
- fridge, kettle
- photocopier
- stock of reference books and materials.

How do I work out my capital allowances?

On the right is an example of how a calculation for capital allowances is made both for studio equipment and a car.

Example of calculation of capital allowances

		Pool	Car	Private 30% on car	Allowance
Year end 5 Apr 96		£	£	£	£
6 Apr 95	Equipment and car introduced	2000	1000		
5 Apr 96	Writing down allowance @ 25%	-500	-250	-75	675
	Tax written down value carried forward	1500	750		
	Capital allowances claimed for the year end 5 Apr 96				675
Year end 5 Apr 97					
6 Apr 96	Tax written down value brought forward	1500	750		
10 Jun 96	Disposal of printer, cost £100 sold for £50	-50			
17 Jul 96	Additions of new easel and lightbox	400			
		1850	750		
5 Apr 97	Writing down allowance @ 25%	-463	-188	-56	595
	Tax written down value carried forward	1387	562		
	Capital allowances claimed for the year end 5 Apr 97				595
Year end 5 Apr 98					
6 Apr 97	Tax written down value brought forward	1387	562		
18 Oct 97	Disposal of car, cost £1,000, sold for £550		-550		
	Balancing allowance on car		-12	-4	8
	Addition of new car		1,200		
		1387	1200		
5 Apr 98	Writing down allowance @ 25%	-347	-300	-90	558
	Tax written down value carried forward	1040	900		
	Capital allowances claimed for the year end 5 Apr 98				566

4 • Tax problem areas

Working at home

If you work at home, there can be problems in agreeing the proportion of domestic expenses which you may claim as a business expense.

Rent

If you rent your home and use one room as a studio, it should be quite easy to agree with the Inland Revenue what proportion of rent you can claim as a deduction in your accounts: either the total rent divided by the total number of rooms in your home, or the total rent apportioned between the average number of hours you work per week divided by the total number of hours in a week (168). This usually equates to 25%. The usual way to agree this when you submit your first set of accounts is to simply notify the Inland Revenue how you have calculated the charge. The Inland Revenue may challenge the costs if they think the basis of calculation unreasonable.

The percentage calculated above can be applied to other costs such as your gas and electricity bills, water rates, etc.

Telephone

Where you only have one telephone line for both business and domestic purposes the best thing to do is to log and monitor your calls. If not, you will have to make an estimate of how much your business calls cost as a proportion of your total telephone costs. The Inland Revenue is usually happy to agree a fairly high proportion of total telephone expenditure on the basis that using the telephone for work during the daytime makes business calls more expensive.

Mortgage

If you own your own house and have a mortgage, then it is not a good idea to try to claim a percentage of your mortgage interest in the same way as rent, mentioned above. This is because if you sold your house, the Inland Revenue could claim that part of it was a business asset and a proportion of it could be liable to Capital Gains Tax.

4 • Tax problem areas

Use of home

What is usual in this situation is to claim an allowance for 'use of your home as a studio'. This is a nominal amount not designed to represent the value of the mortgage, but to cover sundry revenue costs such as extra cleaning, heating, etc. The amount that you could claim would be about £6-7 per week but may vary depending on your circumstances.

Studio mortgage

If you have taken a mortgage specifically to finance the purchase of a studio with associated living accommodation, for example where the studio is in an outbuilding, then it might be worthwhile claiming tax relief on a proportion of the property. This would need to be a specific agreement with the Inland Revenue and you would probably require professional advice. But if you sold the property, the studio on which you had claimed income tax relief would be liable to a Capital Gains Tax charge as a business asset if a profit was made.

Other considerations

Other points to bear in mind when you work from home are local bye-laws which may prohibit you, particularly if your neighbours object.

If you have clients or sub-contractors visiting your home, then you must ensure you have adequate public liability and employee insurance. Also note that if you have domestic insurance, this could be invalidated by you working at home.

If you work from home then technically you may have to consider whether the property should be rated for the uniform business rate. Advice on this matter can be sought from your local council.

Expenditure with a dual purpose

Some items that you buy or own and introduce into the business may be bought for both business and domestic use (dual purpose). A common example is your car.

To agree with the Inland Revenue the proportion of your motor expenses which are tax allowable, you will need to keep a log of all the expenses you incur covering all your petrol, whether business or domestic, insurance, road fund licence, repairs and servicing, parking costs, etc. Any travel between your home and your studio will count as domestic travel but travel to visit clients or to buy materials would all count as business travel.

If you are not able to keep a log, you will have to make a sensible estimate at the end of the year. Estimate what percentage of total mileage was used for business, eg try to average the destination and mileage per week. Remember you have to justify this figure with the Inland Revenue. People who cover long distances to see clients can obviously claim more mileage and claims of 70% to 80% of total expenditure are quite common in these cases.

The Inland Revenue is getting much stricter about claims where you travel a long distance to see a client and can argue you are simply putting yourself in a position to do the work, which counts as private travel rather than a legitimate business expense. As long as you do not actually do the work at the client's premises but return to your studio to do it, then there is a good chance of success with your claim.

Other items where you may have to agree a business use percentage are those on which you are claiming capital allowances such as a stereo (where you are using this part for business and part for pleasure), a camera, a television and video if used for reference purposes, a washing machine where you are working with textiles etc. On such items as televisions, videos, washing machines etc the Inland Revenue will normally only agree between 33% and 50%. For items such as your camera you may well be able to justify a much higher percentage of up to 80% to 90%, but again this would depend on how much you use it for your work and the evidence you can provide, if ever requested, to prove it.

Other areas where you may need to agree a percentage split would be on certain reference materials, and bank charges where you only have one bank account.

The important thing to bear in mind is that there are absolutely no hard and fast rules. For each category of expenditure with a dual purpose you will need to come up with an individual estimate and disclose it to the Inland Revenue for their approval.

Grants & prizes

There are many competition prizes and grants from Government, local authority, charitable and artistic foundations that artists can qualify for. Such is the range in diversity of these and the conditions for successful application for them that to discuss them in detail here would be inappropriate.

All artists should make enquiries to bodies such as their local authority, any local enterprise agency, TEC or LEC, libraries, regional arts boards, the Crafts Council, and regional enterprise agencies about grants which might be available. Also, direct approaches to charitable and artistic foundations can be made when specific projects are in mind.

Most grants are treated as taxable income, particularly grants such as the Enterprise Allowance, Crafts Council equivalent grants and many local authority grants. But it is not possible to generalise because the rules vary according to the grant. It is essential to ask the authority giving the grant their advice on the appropriate tax treatment. The authority should have considered this point and agreed the status of their grants with the relevant taxation authorities. Particular exceptions are grants for educational purposes. These are mostly outside the scope of taxation. So if there is any element of a grant that relates to education it is well worthwhile enquiring about taxation treatment.

Prizes can be more confusing as the term is used in different ways. If you enter a competition (eg an open exhibition) where there is no assurance of a financial gain for yourself and the prize is simply an amount of money given to you as a 'reward' then it's possibly not taxable. But if the 'prize' is something like a competition for a commission (ie competing for a contract) then it's not really a prize and so is taxable. Again ask the prize giving body for advice as it should have sorted out tax status.

To eliminate all doubt, it is essential that all grants and prizes be declared upon the tax return for the year when the grant is paid. In most cases this will simply mean that the grant will be taxed as part of the artist's income for the year in question but, as noted, there are exceptions.

Sponsorship

In almost all cases the receipt of sponsorship by an artist or art organisation is considered by the Inland Revenue to be the receipt of taxable income, and should be treated as if it were any other sale by the artist. This means, if the artist is VAT registered, a VAT invoice must be sent to the sponsoring organisation.

The possible exception with regard to VAT is if the organisation receiving sponsorship is a charity, and the sponsorship does not provide significant benefit to the sponsor, eg their name is not prominently associated with the recipient's activities. Then the sponsorship may be considered to be charitable income and so outside the scope of tax. If this situation can be agreed, the charity should apply VAT to the sponsoring organisation at zero rate, ie no VAT is charged.

To ensure this is the case it is essential that the sponsor is really not seen to obtain much benefit from the charity, ie that the grant is a donation, not to purchase advertising.

Payments to staff & PAYE

see 'PAYE and National Insurance', **16 • Artist as employer**, pages 93-95

This area is covered in more detail in the chapter 'Artist as employer', but you should be aware that if you do pay another person for helping you in your business you need to ascertain whether they are your employee or a sub-contractor.

An artist working for another artist is usually providing services as a sub-contractor, unless the work is full-time or on a regular basis. Extra care must be taken if the sub-contractor works in your studio. For example if a graphic designer employs an illustrator, or an artist in mixed media uses another with a complementary skill to make part of a collage or sculpture, then usually no tax needs to be deducted. If you have another artist who works in your premises under your 'direction and control', or someone to assist you such as a secretary, then they are your employee and you will need to deduct tax and National Insurance.

The Inland Revenue is getting stricter about who is and who is not an employee and if you fail to deduct tax and National Insurance when you should, they can treat the payments you have made as net of tax and ask you for the tax and National Insurance on top. If you are in any doubt you should ask your accountant or the Inland Revenue for advice.

If you pay someone under £58 per week (1995/6) and know that they do not have any other jobs, no tax or National Insurance needs to be deducted provided the person completes forms *P46* and *P15* to state they have no other source of income. These forms can be obtained from the Inland Revenue as part of the PAYE pack the Inland Revenue supply when you ask for a PAYE scheme.

If you do have an employee you must obtain a PAYE scheme from the Inland Revenue and either learn how to do the calculations or ask your accountant to do this for you. The PAYE and National Insurance deducted from your employee's salary has to be paid over to the Inland Revenue either monthly or quarterly.

see 'PAYE and National Insurance', **16 • Artist as employee**, pages 93-95

The detailed calculation of PAYE is beyond the scope of this book, although further detail is given in the chapter 'Artist as employer'. The detailed operation of PAYE is fully described in the Inland Revenue packs supplied with a PAYE scheme. Apply for them in the first instance from your own tax office.

Working abroad

see 'Exporting',
19 • Being VAT-
registered, page 108

If you simply sell your work abroad, then the income should be included in your self-employed accounts in the usual way. The price to include it at is the amount in sterling that you actually get in your bank account. If you sell work abroad and are VAT registered, then the rules are complicated.

If you work abroad for any length of time, this can complicate your tax affairs considerably. It is highly unlikely that you will be able to deal with this situation without professional help. It is always advisable to seek such help before leaving the UK, since it may be possible to simplify your tax affairs by correctly timing the dates of your departure and arrival, as well as to make sure that all the necessary forms are correctly completed.

If you and your parents have always lived in the UK and consider it to be your natural home, then provided that you do not own any property abroad, you are almost certain to be what is known as both 'resident' and 'domiciled' in the UK for tax purposes. As such all income and earnings from anywhere in the world regardless of what you do with them are probably taxable in the UK. They should be included as part of your self-employed accounts or shown on your tax return. If the figures you earn are denominated in a foreign currency, then these should be translated using an appropriate exchange rate.

If tax has been deducted by the overseas country, and there is a double taxation treaty between the UK and that country, then the tax can be offset against the UK tax liability. This is a complicated process and subject to detailed rules. You would need professional advice. There are double taxation treaties between most countries and the UK.

If you are abroad continuously for more than six months in a tax year, or you leave the UK specifically to take up employment abroad, and you own no home in the UK which remains available for you to use while you are abroad, then it may be possible that the Inland Revenue would agree that you became 'non-resident' in the UK on the day you left the country, in which case you may not be liable to UK tax on your overseas earnings. If you remain abroad for a complete tax year you may also become 'non-resident'.

You should be warned that professional help in sorting out residence problems is expensive but unavoidable if you are to keep your affairs in order. It may be worth bearing this cost in mind when you are assessing whether or not the work abroad is worthwhile taking. You should also make sure that you investigate your obligations under the taxation system of the country you are visiting to make sure that you comply with them. This is better done by enquiry in that country unless you use an international firm of accountants.

5 • The Inland Revenue

The Inland Revenue is frequently seen as a distant enemy ready to pounce on very penny they can of your hard earned income. In fact this is not a fair view and in recent years the Inland Revenue has taken steps to become more user friendly, encouraging the self-employed to see them as a sympathetic source of help and advice.

If you are self-employed and on a low income, you may not be able to afford an accountant. In this case you can deal with the Inland Revenue direct. If you are self-employed you will have your tax affairs dealt with by your local office, which makes it much easier to seek advice and develop a relationship with whoever is allocated your case. A file will be kept on you and your affairs and can be referred to when you phone. You will be allocated a schedule D reference number which you should always quote when contacting them by phone or letter.

If you find yourself in difficulties with any aspect of your tax affairs, phone the Inland Revenue direct to ask for advice. If the person answering the phone cannot help ask to speak to some one who can. But remember its not the Inland Revenue's job to minimise your tax liability. They will answer your questions but are unlikely to draw to your attention claims and reliefs which will reduce your tax bill.

Being on time

The Inland Revenue will always view your accounts more favourably if you send them in quite soon after your year end. There are also other good reasons for not allowing your accounts to get out of date.

If you keep up to date you will always know how your business is doing. You will know whether you are making more or less sales than last year and you will know how your money has been spent. If you are making a loss then it may be time to think about your costing structures, or to take other measures to correct the situation. In extreme situations this would mean giving up being a self-employed artist and looking for a job.

Under the present tax system your first year of accounts should be submitted to the Inland Revenue two or three months after your year end. Thereafter you should aim to have your accounts with the Inland Revenue four to five months after your accounting year end. This gives the Inland Revenue plenty of time to agree your accounts and raise correct assessments rather than estimates. This will save you a lot of administration time.

Under the self-assessment system which will take effect from the tax return for the year ended 5 April 1997, accounts for self-employed people with sales income of less than £15,000 (1995/6) will form part of the tax return, and no separate accounts will be required unless the Inland Revenue enquire more closely into your affairs. For those with income above £15,000, the accounts should be submitted along with the tax return. This means that the date that accounts will need to be submitted by will be the same date as the relevant year's tax return. If your accounts are not prepared on time you should estimate your profit and explain why it is an estimate, but do be aware of the risk of interest and penalites. If your year end is a date other than 5 April, be sure not to submit your accounts with the wrong return. You may need professional advice.

You may need your accounts to be prepared for reasons other than agreeing your tax, in which case they should be prepared as soon as possible even if you then wait to submit them to the Inland Revenue with your tax return form.

Enquiries

Under the self-assessment system which is effective from 5 April 1997, the Inland Revenue will have more powers to enquire into tax returns and accounts. No formal agreement to your accounts will be issued and the Inland Revenue will have 12 months from the filing date of the return, 30 September or 31 January, to enquire into any matter or ask for supporting information. This may involve asking for all your accounts records and receipts or checking why a figure of bank interest disagrees with the returns made by the bank. There does not have to be a reason for an enquiry under the new system and it could be entirely random. It is therefore essential to keep books, records and receipts and to retain these. (See the chapters on bookkeeping). It is also important to ensure that you can identify where all sums of money banked into your bank and building society accounts have come from. Any estimates included in your accounts or returns and their basis of calculation should be disclosed with the return. The Inland Revenue procedure for the conduct of enquiries is beyond the scope of this book.

Interest and penalties

Tax in respect of your self-employment is currently due in two equal instalments on 1 January in the year of assessment and 1 July following the year of assessment. If the correct amount of tax has not been paid by 1 July following the year of assessment then any amount underpaid is subject to an interest charge at the official rate of interest which is roughly equivalent to market rates. Interest will run until payment is made.

If the relevant set of accounts forming the basis of the tax liability has not been prepared, then an estimate should be made of the taxable profits and a payment made on account to the Inland Revenue to avoid interest being charged. Under new rules effective from January 1998, a more detailed system of interest and penalties will be introduced, with surcharges for late payment as well as interest. Under this system you will be much more likely to pay interest charges than at present.

If you have been trading for several years and not informed the Inland Revenue or paid any tax in respect of your self-employment, you can be charged interest on the tax when you do finally pay, and also receive penalties for failure to notify chargeability to tax and failure to submit a Tax Return. This is charged under the penalty provisions for negligence or fraud. The penalty where chargeability has not been notified can be a maximum of the actual tax liability for the year, ie you may pay twice as much in total as the tax liability if the maximum penalty is charged.

However, if the Inland Revenue makes a mistake which works against you, fails to repay tax owed to you or takes an unreasonably long time to repay tax owed, you can make a complaint. Write to the head of the Inland Revenue department dealing with your affairs. If you still feel you have not been treated fairly contact the Inland Revenue Adjudicator. If tax owed to you is not paid back on time you may be able to claim interest.

Multiple sources of income

A lot of freelance artists, to support their work as artists and pay their living costs, have to do other work. This may include teaching or casual work such as working behind a bar or in shops. If this is the case you will have two different sources of income: firstly your freelance artist income and secondly your other work which will normally have suffered a deduction for PAYE and National Insurance as an employment.

see 3 • **Tax and self-employment**, pages 19-33

To calculate your overall tax liability for a given tax year you first need to calculate the taxable income figure based on your accounts. It will not always be the amount earned in the accounts for the same period, but the amount which falls into that tax year as adjusted in the tax computation. This must be added to your income from your employment. In other words you are taxed on the total amount you earn in a tax year – self-employment income plus employment income. It is probable that there would have been some tax deducted from employment income and this can be offset against your overall tax liability. The PAYE deduction, plus the amount of tax you have paid on account of your self-employed tax liability for that year, will give you a net difference which will be either extra tax that you owe or a tax refund owing to you.

see 'The tax return form', 3 • **Tax and self-employment**, pages 25-27

If you are due a tax refund then you will be able to claim this when you do your tax return. To support the refund claim you will need to let the Inland Revenue have your *P60* certificate of pay and deductions from your employment, or your *P45* if you have left the job, or the last pay slip you receive in the tax year. The Inland Revenue tends to be much more awkward about making a refund if it has not got either the *P60* or *P45*. It is important to keep such documents safely.

You may have had more than one teaching or casual job in the year as well as your freelance artist income. If this is so, the calculation is done in exactly the same way, except you now have an extra source of income to add to the previous two.

The above calculations would usually be sent to the Inland Revenue with your income tax return. If you have an accountant they will deal with this for you.

The Inland Revenue find multiple sources of income difficult to handle, and the likelihood that they will get your affairs right first time is quite low. If you are due a refund this may take some time to be processed, because the district which deals with your freelance artist income is unlikely to be the same as that where the tax has been deducted on your casual or teaching earnings, and the two districts will need to liaise.

It is worth checking all assessments very carefully and, if you are in any doubt, appeal against the assessment and ask the Inland Revenue to explain their calculations. If you are trying to chase the Inland Revenue up, the best thing is to telephone them but always submit all claims in writing as well and, very importantly, keep a photocopy.

The figures below show the overall calculation of income tax for a year with multiple sources of income. You will see from the examples that the three sources of income for the tax year to 5 April 1996 are added together, and from this figure the personal allowance is deducted. The tax on this net income is compared with the tax already paid and the difference is due to the Inland Revenue. You will see that, where the person is only entitled to the single personal allowance, and because no tax has been deducted on the bookshop income, they actually owe a further £478.75 of income tax. Where they are entitled to a married couple's allowance, this tax is reduced to £220.75.

You should be aware that the more sources of income you have, particularly of a casual nature, and the more you stop and start these jobs, then the more complicated your affairs will be. It is therefore most important that you keep all your payslips, because all of these sources of income will need to be disclosed on your tax return to enable the overall tax calculation to be agreed.

Married person claiming the married couples allowance – Year to 5 Apr 96

	INCOME £	TAX £
Freelance Artist Income (based on accounts to 31 Mar 96)	6000	500.00
Teaching income, Any Town Art College	3500	875.00
P Jones Book Shop	2080	0.00
	11580	1375.00
Less: Personal Allowance	-3525	
	8055	
Tax Due: £3200 @ 20%	640.00	
£4855 @ 25%	1213.75	
	1853.75	
Less: Married Couples Allowance @15%	-258.00	
	1595.75	
Less: Tax Paid	1375.00	
Tax Due	220.75	

Single Person – Year to 5 Apr 96

	INCOME £	TAX £
Freelance Artist Income (based on accounts to 31 Mar 94)	6000	500.00
Teaching income, Any Town Art College	3500	875.00
P Jones Book Shop	2080	0.00
	11580	1375.00
Less: Personal Allowance	-3525	
	8055	
Tax Due: £3200 @ 20%	640.00	
£4855 @ 25%	1213.75	
	1853.75	
Less: Tax Paid	1375.00	
Tax Due	478.75	

6 • National Insurance

There are four different sorts of National Insurance:

- **Class 1** which you pay as an employed person
- **Class 2** which is the self-employed contribution at £5.75 per week (1995/6)
- **Class 3** which is a voluntary contribution of a similar amount to Class 2 made, even when there is no necessity to pay, to protect a right to receive such benefits as an old age pension in the future
- **Class 4** which is National Insurance paid by self-employed people with profits in excess of £6,640 (1995/6). Payment is at 7.3% of profits in excess of £6,640 up to an upper earnings limit. Tax relief is obtained on half the sum paid. This is collected as part of your overall tax demand and is due at the same time as tax on your self-employed income tax.

If you are an employee, Class 1 National Insurance will automatically be deducted if you are over the earnings limit, which is currently £58 per week (1995/6). Class 2 National Insurance is paid if you think that you will make profits in excess of £3,260 a year (1995/6). Class 3 National Insurance contributions enable you to satisfy entitlement to basic retirement pensions, widow's payment and widows' pensions. They are for people who are unable to create an entitlement by being employed or self-employed. They can also be useful for those paying Class 1 or Class 2 National Insurance but who for a particular year failed to make sufficient contributions. Class 4 National Insurance will be automatically calculated as part of your tax assessment. It does not give rise to any entitlement to benefits.

see 'The Department of Social Security', 2 • Starting to trade, page 14

The only usual type of National Insurance that you may be able to get an exception for is the Class 2 National Insurance. If you believe that you will earn profits of under £3,260 then you should speak to the Department of Social Security and make sure that you complete the application for an exception.

see 'The Department of Social Security', 2 • Starting to trade, page 14

It is also possible to claim exception from Class 2 and Class 4 liabilities if you pay the maximum rate of Class 1 contributions. If you believe this to be the case for you, consult with the DSS or your accountant.

If you are in receipt of Enterprise Allowance or grant from your TEC then this does not count as income for the purposes of Class 2 National Insurance. It does count for the purposes of calculating any liability to Class 4 National Insurance, when Enterprise Allowance is added on top of your other freelance earnings.

If you are a freelance artist, but also have other sources of either teaching or casual earnings where Class 1 National Insurance is deducted at source, and you also pay the basic Class 2 stamp, you will be paying double the amount of National Insurance. There is no way to prevent this unless maximum Class 1 National Insurance contributions are paid, when you may apply for exception from liability to Class 2 National Insurance (unless you can apply for this exception anyway because of small earnings).

This is a rather unfair part of the system because, even if you double-pay, you will not get a double benefit. Paying the Class 1 National Insurance may entitle you to some unemployment benefit, the earnings-related part of other benefits and industrial injuries disablement benefit, but overall these advantages may not compensate for paying National Insurance twice.

7 • Benefits

by **Sharon McKee**
with additional
material by
Debbie Duffin

Many artists qualify for state benefits because they are in a category of people who on average have quite low earnings, or have periods where, because they are working on a long-term project, they have no money coming in.

You may find it difficult to get any benefit if the Department of Employment will not recognise that you are unemployed because you are an artist. But you do not have to be unemployed to qualify for all Social Security benefits. Some you can claim if you are self-employed, working part-time, or on a low wage.

Claiming benefits can be complex for artists, particularly if your income and/or employment comes from a variety of sources and at irregular intervals. The regulations governing eligibility are designed for people with more conventional occupations and working patterns, and while the same rules apply to all claimants, individual departments may interpret the rules slightly differently and have different attitudes to those who do not readily 'fit in'.

The way you present your case may partly determine the outcome, so take the attitude that the department is a service you are entitled to make use of, and that it is there to help. If you are self-employed and on a low income it may help to present yourself as a one-person, small business. This puts you in a more easily definable category; it also helps you argue a case for being assessed on your 'profit', ie income less expenses, rather than your gross income (bearing in mind the maximum number of hours you can work and still claim benefits, as well as fulfilling other requirements – see below).

When claiming benefits you will find it easier to put your case if you are fully informed of the rules governing the benefit system. When you first sign on, always ask for any leaflets available explaining the benefit you are applying for.

When reading through the information, make a note of any areas of potential conflict between the regulations and your working life. Armed with information you can then ask the necessary questions to clarify your position and gain the best possible advice from the benefit office.

In the first instance you will probably be dealing with a relatively junior member of staff, who may not have all the information necessary, and will almost certainly not be used to dealing with unusual cases. If you feel you are not being given a fair hearing, need more information or advice, or simply want to discuss your situation with someone more senior, don't hesitate to ask to speak to a supervisor or manager.

This chapter does not purport to be a comprehensive guide to all benefits which you may claim. Two very useful guides are leaflets *FB2 Which Benefit?* and *NI196 Social Security Benefit Rates,* which give up-to-date guidance and rates of a wide range of benefits, which may alter in April each year. Further details can be obtained from the offices of the Department of Social Security, your Citizens' Advice Bureau or Unemployment Benefit Office, the addresses of which can be found in your local telephone directory.

The majority of National Insurance contributions is paid into the National Insurance Fund, out of which contributory benefits are paid. The remainder is paid into the Redundancy Fund and the National Health Service. The class of National Insurance you pay will depend upon your status of employment. When you are not working, for instance if you are sick or unemployed, you can sometimes apply for credits instead of having to pay contributions. These credits can help you qualify for some benefits.

Other useful guides
• **NP28** More than just one job: your class 1 NI contributions
• **NI222** National Insurance for examiners, teachers and instructors
• **NI27A** National Insurance for people with small earnings from self-employment
• **NI41** National Insurance for self-employed people

Contributory benefits include:

• Unemployment Benefit

• Sickness Benefit

• Invalidity Benefit, including pension and allowance

• Retirement Pension

• State Maternity Allowance

• Widow's Benefit

General table of benefits you can be eligible for depending on whether you are employed or self-employed, but remember that these benefits are all contributory. Your eligibility will depend upon your level of National Insurance contributions.

Eligibility for contributory benefits

BENEFIT	EMPLOYED	SELF-EMPLOYED
Sickness Benefit	yes	yes
Statutory Sick Pay	yes	no
Invalidity Benefit	yes	no*
Statutory Maternity Pay	yes	no
Maternity Allowance	yes	yes
RetirementPension	yes	yes
Widow's Benefit	yes	yes
Unemployment Benefit	yes	no*

*a self-employed person may be eligible for these benefits if they have paid enough National Insurance contributions during the period on which eligibility is assessed (see below).

Non-contributory benefits
• Child Benefit
• One-parent Benefit

Means tested, non-contributory benefits
• Income Support
• Family Credit

The main benefits you are likely to claim include:

Unemployment Benefit

• **FB9** Unemployed
• **N12** Unemployment Benefit

This is a weekly flat rate, which increases for any adult dependant the claimant may have. Eligibility depends on the claimant's contribution record. Other conditions include:

• the claimant must be fit for work and available for work;
• show s/he is actively seeking work; and
• must not place unreasonable restrictions on the type of work they will accept.

It is paid for the first year only of any spell of unemployment and will not be paid for the first three days of unemployment.

You may be disqualified from receiving the benefit for up to 26 weeks in certain cases, eg if you left a job voluntarily or were dismissed due to misconduct.

You must register your claim immediately as benefit will not normally be paid for days of unemployement prior to the claim.

Income Support

• **IS1** Income Support

May be claimed in conjunction with Unemployment Benefit or if you are on a low wage, or if you have no money coming in but are not eligible for Unemployment Benefit. Income Support is supposed to pay the difference between an individual or family's weekly net income and the amount required to meet their assessed needs (this includes basic living expenses, some special additional costs and certain housing costs).

You will not be eligible for Income Support if you have £8000 or more capital, ie savings; if you have over £3000, the amount of income support will be reduced. If you are married or living with someone, only one partner may make a claim, as a family will be addressed as a unit. In order to receive Income Support you must still be fit for work, available for and actively seeking work.

Housing Benefit and Council Tax Benefit

• **RR1** Housing Benefit

These two benefits can be claimed if you are unemployed or on a low income. Assessment for Housing Benefit depends upon how much rent you pay, who you live with and the difference between your income and your assessed needs. Eligibility for Council Tax Benefit is assessed in a similar way and you can also claim if you are an owner/occupier. If you have more than £3000 capital this may affect how much Housing Benefit and Council Tax Benefit you receive.

Family Credit

• **FC1** Family Credit

This is a weekly payment to a family with at least one child, with additional payments for each child. It is a non-contributory benefit, dependent on the claimant's net weekly income and capital.

At least one adult of the family must be in full-time (16 hours a week or more) remunerative work (this includes self-employment). They will be assessed for a twenty-six-week period, after which they can seek a further award. Capital over £3000 will affect the amount you receive, if you have over £8000 capital you will not receive Family Credit.

One Parent Benefit

• **CH11** One Parent Benefit

This is single flat rate payment, not affected by the number of children. The claimant does not have to be the child's parent but they must live alone and not be cohabiting.

When on Enterprise Allowance

Enterprise Allowance is a weekly flat-rate allowance, and participants also receive free business counselling. The scheme is handled in England and Wales by local TECs (Training Enterprise Councils) in Scotland by LECs (Local Enterprise Councils), and in Northern Ireland by Local Enterprise Development Units. The names they give it, and the way they operate it differ around the country. Basically the allowance is given for from six months to over a year to set up a new approved business venture. An artist would need to present a viable business proposition to have a reasonable chance of receiving Enterprise Allowance. Some enterprise councils accept 'being an artist' as a viable business but most don't. So you may need to describe yourself, and your activity in some other way.

To qualify you usually must have been unemployed for at least eight weeks (though TECs differ in these rules) and in receipt of unemployment benefit or income support at the time of application, unless you have been on a training programme.

Applicants must also have at least £1000 to invest, and agree to work full time, ie more than thirty six hours per week. The £1000 can be a loan or an overdraft guarantee. It is usually alright to repay the loan or cancel the overdraft as soon as you set up in business.

Applications can also be considered for cooperatives, partnerships or limited companies.

While receiving Enterprise Allowance:

- Income Tax – the allowance is intended to supplement takings, and is taxable as a business receipt; as self-employed, the recipient will be liable for income tax under Schedule D. Returns should be submitted to the local Inspector of Taxes.

see **6 • National Insurance**, pages 46-47

- National Insurance – the recipient will not be liable to pay Class 2 contributions but may be liable to Class 4. This means if you expect to make a profit of less than £3260 (1995/6) in addition to your 'income' from Enterprise Allowance you can claim exception from Class 2 National Insurance payments by getting leaflet *CA02*. However it may not be wise to write this into your business plan for the TEC as it implies a lack of faith in your earning cpacity.

- Other benefits – while receiving Enterprise Allowance you are not entitled to other Social Security benefits; if you are ill, the allowance will be paid for up to eight weeks, but if sickness benefit is claimed then the allowance will be stopped. You can, however, claim Family Credit and Housing Benefit.

When self-employed

Income Support, Family Credit, Housing Benefit and Council Tax Benefit can all be claimed even if you are self-employed, providing you fulfil the standard prerequisites. Assessment as to whether you qualify for these benefits is similar for all four. Your income will be taken into account when judging if it needs to be supplemented by benefits: earnings, benefits, maintenance and any 'other' will be calculated into a weekly basis. Any capital over £3000 is regarded as 'income'. If you are self-employed, or work irregularly, your income may vary from week to week and you will need to make a case for an average income being used for assessment. The period over which the average is calculated will need to be negotiated with your local office. Always calculate your income based on your profit (that is income less expenses) rather than your gross income – otherwise you will receive less benefit than you are entitled to. Income Support is taxable under Schedule E, while Family Credit is tax-free.

see 6 • National Insurance, pages 46-47

National Insurance Contributions

see 6 • National Insurance, pages 46-47

When you are self-employed you normally pay Class 2 and Class 4 contributions unless there are certain exemptions. Class 3 is a voluntary contribution, which anyone can pay. It is worth considering this if your contribution record is not sufficient to qualify you for benefits which you feel you may need to claim in the future. If you are on a low income you can apply for exception from paying NI contributions. However this may affect your eligibility for some benefits.

Your local Social Security Officer can find out the level of your contribution record, and give advice on what benefits this entitles you to and whether it would be worth paying Class 3 to make yourself eligible for others.

Class 2 counts towards entitlement to certain contributory benefits, but not unemployment benefit.

Pensions

• NP46 A guide to Retirement Pension • NI92 Giving up your Retirement Pension to earn extra • FB6 Retiring

The basic pension is a flat rate, part of the contributory state Retirement Pension. This is paid to anyone whose contribution record satisfies certain contribution conditions. Self-employed and voluntary contributions can be counted for this purpose. State pensions are not high and it may be worthwhile joining a private pension scheme.

Sickness

• **NI116** Sickness Benefit
• **NI253** Ill and unable to work
• **FB28** Sick or disabled

If you are self-employed you cannot qualify for Statutory Sick Pay unless you are also employed and earnings are above the lower earnings level for National Insurance contribution purposes. But you may be entitled to Sickness Benefit, for up to 28 weeks, if you have paid enough Class 1 or Class 2 contributions. You cannot claim Sickness Benefit for the first four days of illness.

Maternity

• **FB8** Babies and Benefit

If you are not actually employed, you cannot qualify for Statutory Maternity Pay, but you will probably be able to claim Maternity Allowance, which can be paid for 18 weeks, starting from the 11th week before your baby is due, or later if you are still working. To be eligible for Maternity Allowance, you will have had to pay enough Class 1 or Class 2 contributions.

Unemployment

A self-employed person may be able to claim Unemployment Benefit depending on the following criteria:

• you have paid sufficient Class 1 contributions in the past, while an employee, to at least receive the reduced rate of Unemployment Benefit. This rules out a person who was wholly self-employed during the tax year to which the second contribution condition (below) relates.

• you must be prepared to work as an employee.

• you must have paid Class 1 contributions in either of the last two tax years, prior to the calendar year of claim.

• you must have paid or been credited with Class 1 contributions in both of the last two tax years, ending in the calendar year before the unemployment began.

Normally to qualify for unemployment benefit you have to be capable of work, unemployed and available for work and 'actively seeking work' but it can also be claimed for a 'period of interruption of employment'.

This period of interruption has its own definition. Any two days of unemployment separated by no more than five clear days (not including Sundays) can be linked to form a period of interruption of employment. Any number of days can be linked together in this way, provided they are not isolated by more than five days. These days may be linked together with other such days, providing that two periods are no more than eight weeks apart. You may be able to claim

• **FB26** Voluntary and part-time workers

while working part-time, eg part-time teaching. Ask at you local Unemployment Benefit Office or advice centre.

Lower earnings limit

If earnings are below this level, neither employer nor employee is liable to pay Class 1 contributions.

The LEL for 1995/6 is £58 per week. If a person has more than one job, each earnings is usually treated separately for contribution purposes. Occasionally the law will determine that they be aggregated, eg if a person has more than one contract with the same employer.

Other help

As well as the other benefits listed at the beginning if you are on a low income, help can also be gained to pay for such things as dental treatment, sight tests, prescriptions, milk and vitamins. Legal aid is available and you may, through Social Security, have access to a social fund loan, although money from this is often difficult to obtain, inadequate and has to be repaid.

Medical and Social Security abroad

• **T1** A travellers guide to health
• **NI38** Social Security abroad
• **SA29** Your Social Security and pension rights in the EC

The UK has medical care and Social Security agreements with some other countries which may help you to get treatment and benefits while you are abroad.

Your Social Security benefits can be affected if you leave the UK for more than a few weeks. For example, if you or your child leave for more than eight weeks, you usually won't get child benefit or one-parent benefit.

Appeals

If you feel you have been unfairly treated and have been turned down for a benefit you believe you are entitled to, or think you are entitled to more money than you have been awarded, you are well within your rights to make an appeal.

• **NI246** How to Appeal

Notice must be given in writing, within three months of the decision, to your local social security office (preferably the one which made the decision you are appealing against). You can get a form from them. Citizens' Advice Bureaux, local authority Social Security Departments and claimants' unions can all offer advice.

Information
Leaflets are available explaining each benefit in detail, these can normally be obtained from your local Department of Social Security. Some may be available at main post offices. Conditions and payment levels change from year to year, the information in this chapter serves as a guide and you should always obtain relevant information before making a claim.

Support group

- **Child Poverty Action Group**, 1-5 Bath Street, London EC1V 9PY, 0171 253 6569. Runs Citizens' Rights Office and publishes guides to Social Security and Welfare benefits.

8 • VAT and the artist

Who should read this chapter

It is essential that everyone who is engaged in a business on their own account, whatever its legal structure, understands the nature and importance of Value Added Tax (VAT) if they are to avoid some of the worst pitfalls any business can come across. Whether you are VAT-registered or not, and whether you need to be so or not, it is essential that you read this chapter.

This chapter doesn't deal with the detail of how to complete a VAT return, which is covered in the chapter 'VAT accounts'. This only needs to be read if you are VAT-registered.

see **20 • VAT accounts**, pages 114-133

When you need to register

VAT is a tax on the chargeable supplies made by a VAT-registered trader. A chargeable supply is a sale of just about anything by a self-employed person, a partnership, or limited company. But there are exceptions as specified in the chapter 'Being VAT-registered'. In addition to those it is important to note that any receipts a self-employed person receives from employment do not have to be added to sales for VAT purposes. But, if a self-employed person runs more than one trade, the sales of all have to be added together to determine the total chargeable supplies.

see 'Exempt (not liable to VAT)' **19 • Being VAT-registered**, page 109

When the level of chargeable supplies made by an artist, whether a sole trader, partnership or limited company, exceed limits laid down in law, then it is essential that the artist registers for VAT. The limits increase annually. Those below are for 1995/6. VAT registration will be necessary if:

- an artist has made cumulative sales of £46,000 in a period of twelve months or less, ending on the last day of a month, when they have to register for VAT within 30 days of the end of the month in which this event occurs.
- the artist expects to make sales of more than £46,000 within the next 30 days, when, if they are not already registered, they must become so immediately.

Registering

To register for VAT, telephone your local VAT office, which will be found in the telephone directory under Customs & Excise. Ask for the registration department, tell them you want to register for VAT and they will send you form *VAT 1*. If you have any problems in completing it, do not hesitate to telephone them for assistance, which they should provide. Alternatively, if you have an accountant, contact them immediately if you exceed the registration limits and be sure they register you. But be warned, Customs & Excise are of the view that if your accountant fails to act on your behalf then you may still be liable to fines for not registering on time, so ensure that your accountant really does do what you ask.

Warning

If you do not register for VAT in accordance with the above rules and within the time limits specified, then Customs & Excise will fine you and the range of defences available to any fine they impose is extremely limited. They do not have to take you to court to impose the fine. In effect, when Customs & Excise prosecute they are the prosecution, the judge, the jury, and the beneficiary of the fines paid. The odds will be stacked against you. These fines are:

- **Up to 9 months late with registration** – you will be fined 10% of the amount of VAT you should have paid Customs & Excise during this period, and you will also be required to pay the VAT you should have charged to customers, even though you did not and they will probably never now pay it to you. Effectively the fine is therefore about 19% of your sales.
- **Between 10 and 18 months late** – the fine increases to 20% of the VAT you should have paid to Customs & Excise, plus the VAT itself, totalling about 21% of your sales during this period.

- **More than 18 months late** – the fine becomes 30% of the VAT owing for the period plus the VAT itself, an effective fine of approximately 23% of sales.
- If by any chance any of the above fines is less than £50, then there is a minimum fine of £50.

Because these payments are fines you will get no income tax relief on them. So, although you might have to pay a fine of almost 20% of your income you would still have to pay income tax on that sum as well, meaning that the real cost of the fine is even higher.

The net effect of these fines is that you cannot afford to ever be late with VAT registration, and you must always bear the need for it in mind if you are not registered.

Voluntary registration

The artist needs be very wary with regard to pricing work when VAT is involved. If their customer is a business then, as referred to in the preceding paragraph, they need not worry too much about adding VAT because a business will expect the price to be quoted without VAT on the assumption they will be charged it and be able to reclaim it from Customs & Excise.

An individual who is a customer cannot reclaim the VAT and as such it is part of the true cost to them. So, if they have set a budget to spend, the VAT has to come out of this and effectively can be considered to be a charge upon the artist. The amount of this charge can be worked out in the same way as for the amount of VAT included in a receipt where the VAT is not specified, ie the gross price (including VAT) is multiplied by 7 and divided by 47. For example, if the artist believes they can charge £470 inclusive of VAT, because that is what the private buyer will pay, to find the VAT £470 must be multiplied by 7 and divided by 47, giving an answer of £70. The result of this is that, of the amount the artist believes can be obtained from the paying public, £400 is available to themselves for the work done and £70 is paid in tax.

There is an important point in here. For many artists VAT registration means that, because they can only charge a fixed price for their work, they are not in the position of a normal business; for the artist, VAT registration often means that effectively they pay the VAT, not the customer, which would be the normal case. So most artists are best advised to avoid VAT registration until they are legally required to register.

It is always possible to voluntarily register for VAT if it can be shown that financial hardship would result from not being registered, even though the sales of the business did not otherwise justify it. Except for someone with a particularly heavy expenditure on materials or equipment on which VAT is charged, which is unlikely to be the case for artists, this is not normally recommended. The only normal exception would be those with high material inputs into their work who often sell to business customers.

Of course, once sales exceed the VAT registration limit, registration is compulsory. It is worth noting that if an artist has registered for VAT and their sales then fall below the limit, they may apply to be de-registered. This may be worthwhile, but care must be taken to ensure that re-registration is not required at sometime in the future.

Cash accounting

A final point with regard to VAT registration. Two methods of VAT accounting are allowed in law: the 'normal' basis and the 'cash' basis. The latter is only available to smaller businesses making sales of less than £350,000 a year. The amount of record-keeping required for the cash basis is rather lower than the normal basis. Also a considerable advantage is that, under the cash basis of accounting, VAT on sales is not owed to Customs & Excise until the customer has paid. So it is very strongly recommended that small businesses use the cash basis of accounting for VAT. It is that form of accounting that is considered in this book.

Galleries

VAT can cause problems in the relationship between an artist and a gallery taking work on a sale or return basis, ie not buying the work in order to resell it.

If the artist is not VAT-registered but the gallery is:

- The gallery is entitled to add VAT to the sale price of your work because the general public will not be aware that you own it and not the gallery. As such the final sale price will be inclusive of VAT. This means that the net sales price on which a commission will be operated will be the sale price less the VAT.

- When charging you commission the gallery will be entitled to add VAT, ie if you have agreed a commission rate of, say, 25% then they can add on 17.5% VAT to this 25% making the charge in total 29.375%.

The way in which this works in practice is, for example, if you place a piece of work at a net selling price of £200 with a gallery and with an agreed commission rate of 25%:

- the price the customer will pay will be £200 plus VAT, ie £235

- the price on which commission should be charged is the net selling price, ie £200

- the commission that you will pay will be £50, but to this will be added VAT at 17.5%, ie £8.75, making a total commission payment of £58.75

- you will in effect receive from the gallery £200 less the commission plus VAT on the commission, ie £200 less £58.75, being £141.25.

If both artist and gallery are VAT-registered:
In this case you must also ensure that the transaction is properly recorded for VAT purposes in your own books. So, in addition to receiving notification from the gallery that the work is sold, and receiving a copy of their invoice for the commission (including VAT which you can reclaim from Customs & Excise), you must bill them for the value of the sale that has been passed on to the customer, ie you must raise an invoice for £200 plus VAT to the gallery which they can match up with the bill that they will effectively have to raise from them to the customer. In this way VAT paid by the customer is effectively declared by you as your output VAT and the VAT charged to you by the gallery is declared as input VAT. Following the above example of a work with a net selling price of £200:

- the price the customer pays is £200 plus VAT, ie £235

- the price on which the commission is charged is the net selling price, ie £200

- the commission the artist pays the gallery is £50, but to this the gallery adds VAT @ 17.5%, ie £8.75, making a total commission payment of £58.75

• the amount the artist receives is not £141.75 as in the first example but £176.25, which is the difference between the gross selling price of £235 and the gross commission of £58.75. The artist receives the additional £25 because it is the responsibility of the artist to pay this to Customs & Excise, rather than that of the gallery.

Some galleries have what is termed a 'self-billing' arrangement to make all this simpler, and this enables them to raise the bill from the artist to the gallery for the sale of a picture on your behalf. Many artists will find this convenient, but it is essential to take advice either from Customs & Excise or an accountant before entering into such a scheme to ensure that the complications of it are understood. If you enter into a self-billing arrangement and have given your written consent, you must never raise a bill to the other person in the arrangement but should accept that the information they provide to you constitutes your invoices and should be declared on your VAT return as recorded by them.

see 'Problems with galleries', **9 •**
Customers, page 71

An alternative arrangement

The above notes cover the normal attitude of Customs and Excise to galleries. However, an alternative arrangement is possible. This requires a contract between the gallery and the artist which makes it absolutely clear that the gallery is selling the work as an agent of the artist. Additionally, the gallery must make it clear on all the documentation supplied to the eventual customer that they are acting as agent only, and that the sale is between the customer and the artist. In this case the sale to the end customer is made by the artist, not the gallery, and VAT is only added to the sale price if the artist is VAT-registered. If the artist is not VAT-registered, VAT is not added. The gallery, if registered, will add VAT to their commission charged to the artist.

For the non-VAT-registered artist there is advantage in attempting to adopt this form of arrangement, because it means that the sale price of their work is relatively lower, and therefore more attractive. The disadvantage is that Customs and Excise do not like it. Because of the risk associated with this arrangement, it is not recommended that any artist or gallery should operate in this way without first seeking professional advice and preferably having agreed the arrangement and associated documentation with Customs and Excise in advance of its use.

9 • Customers

Sales invoices

For further information on approaches to selling and sales administration, see AN Publications' *Selling*, and for sales contracts see *Selling Contracts*; details given at the end of this book

Whenever you make a sale of your work it is advisable that you raise a sales invoice. This can either be on your own headed notepaper, in which case it is essential to keep a carbon copy for your own records, or in a duplicate/triplicate invoice book that can be bought from many stationers. An example of a sales invoice, with all the information required both by law and, in practical terms, for a person who is VAT-registered, is shown on the next page.

This assumes the person making the sale is a sole trader. In the case of a partnership or a limited company it is highly advisable that the invoice be on the firm or company's own headed notepaper. Variations on this are possible, particularly if you are not VAT-registered, as the amount of information needed is reduced because the law is not so specific. If you use a duplicate book it may well be worthwhile having a rubber stamp with your name and address, your credit terms and also details of to whom payment is to be made.

Without a copy invoice it is virtually impossible to pursue your debt if somebody does not pay. It is also extremely difficult to accurately account for your sales. For both reasons it is essential that a copy is kept. In addition, if the invoices are written up in your accounts books very soon after they are raised, you have a record independent of the copy invoices of who owes you money.

see 'Sales and income', 17 • Keeping account, page 97

Terms of trade

It is important to decide on what conditions you are willing to trade with people. In essence – are you going to provide credit, or do you require cash payment before they can have the items they have purchased? If you are working on a commission, the terms of trade will inevitably have to incorporate the terms under which you will be paid as the work progresses. The most important things about the terms of trade are:

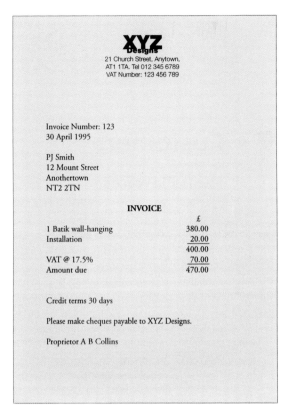

For VAT purposes your sales invoices should show:
- date (tax point)
- your VAT number
- your name and address
- the customer's name and address
- a description of the goods or services
- the amount before VAT (net value)

If you are not VAT registered:
- folow points to above but exclude all references to VAT

- you decide what they are
- agree these with your customer
- put them in writing
- you should stick to them
- if the customer does not stick to them, you let them know.

If you are selling to members of the general public, of whom you have very little knowledge, it is advisable that your terms of trade are that cash payment is made in full before you part with your work. Be warned that a cheque for a sum in excess of the cheque guarantee card limit can be dishonoured by a bank, so it is not equivalent to cash. You are entitled to defer supply of your work until the cheque has cleared.

Giving credit

If you are supplying to large, apparently reputable companies, you may have to make sales on credit terms. In most circumstances there is no reason to provide credit terms in excess of thirty days. This period is common because it normally takes a large company several weeks to process an invoice and raise a cheque for settlement. As most large companies try to abuse credit terms anyway and take longer than the period officially provided, to be more generous is simply inviting them to take greatly-extended credit.

Be wary before providing anyone with credit. In essence this means that you part with your work before you receive your money. If for any reason they refuse to pay, or are unable to pay, it is often difficult for you to recover your work. You are therefore at risk and should only provide credit if you are fairly confident about the good reputation of the person. There are credit agencies you can ask your bank to make enquiries of, but it is often more appropriate to ask the company who has requested credit for details of its bankers so you

Example of a letter asking for a credit reference

XYZ Designs
21 Church Street, Anytown,
AT1 1TA. Tel 012 345 6789

1 April 1995

The Manager
Midshires Bank PLC
High street
Anothertown

Dear Sir

ART LIMITED

We are currently considering providing credit terms to the above named company whom we understand to be a customer of your bank. It is likely that we shall be making sales to this company of approximately £500 per month and that at any time they might have credit outstanding to us of approximately £1000.

We would be grateful if you would inform us as to whether you consider that they will be good for debt for this amount.

Yours faithfully

A B Collins

can make a direct enquiry of credit-worthiness to that bank. It may also be appropriate to send such an enquiry to a trade supplier who is already making sales to the company.

The replies you receive will not be specific and rarely condemnatory. But, if they say very little or appear to be evasive, be warned. This normally means that the writer has a very low opinion of the company in question. In that case, request cash before delivery.

Commissions

When accepting a commission for work it is even more important you agree the terms of trade with the client. The range of terms available is so vast it is impossible to generalise. But it is advisable to agree the total fee and that payment be made in instalments. The first such instalment would normally be paid on the commission being signed, ie at the outset. The percentage paid at this stage would depend on how long the commission is to last. If it is of fairly short duration this might be of a reasonably high percentage, such as 40% to 50%. If the commission is likely to last for a reasonable period of time, then a further percentage payment might be made during the course of the commission period. For example, if the commission lasts six months, it would be quite reasonable to have a second payment after three months. The client might at this stage have an option to review progress. In either case, a substantial part of the balance of the commission value would be payable upon completion and supply of the work. By this stage at least 90% should have been paid. It might be appropriate to leave a small balance owing for payment about 30 days after the work has been delivered. This is often appropriate if the artist needs to take part in the hanging or placing of the work, or other aspects of final display. It is usually seen by the client as a small retention fee to ensure they do not settle in full until they are finally satisfied with the work. Nonetheless, an agreed date for payment should be determined in advance.

Be warned, you should try to keep this balance of the fee as low as possible. It is the one bit over which the client may eventually wish to haggle, so the smaller it is the less you have to lose. Written agreement in advance always limits the scope for subsequent argument and you should have defined, as clearly as possible and in advance what you mean by the client being satisfied with the work so that they do not have too much room to argue. The client not liking the work is certainly no reason for non-payment. Remember, they would not have given you the commission if they did not like your work. Do not believe this necessarily involves lawyers and other such matters. An agreement written in straightforward English and signed by both parties to a commission arrangement is often as useful as the most convoluted legal contract. If, however, the value of the contract is very high and your potential loss likely to be financially crippling, the involvement of a professional adviser might be sensible.

Debt recovery

If your terms of trade are that everyone has to pay in cash or by cleared cheque before they can receive your work, then debt recovery will never be a problem. In this case, consider yourself lucky. If you do supply on credit terms, you will inevitably come across someone who tries to abuse these terms and take extended credit from you, or simply tries to avoid paying.

This statement refers to the invoice on page 64. It shows the information that should be sent to a customer when the time comes for the to pay.

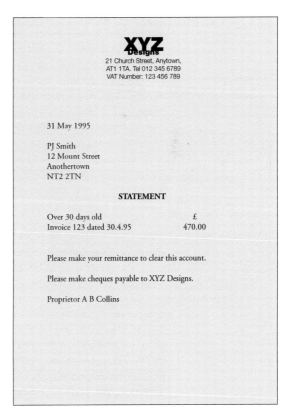

XYZ
Designs
21 Church Street, Anytown,
AT1 1TA. Tel 012 345 6789
VAT Number: 123 456 789

31 May 1995

PJ Smith
12 Mount Street
Anothertown
NT2 2TN

STATEMENT

	£
Over 30 days old	
Invoice 123 dated 30.4.95	470.00

Please make your remittance to clear this account.

Please make cheques payable to XYZ Designs.

Proprietor A B Collins

For further information on contracts for work undertaken on commissions, see AN Publication's *Commission Contracts;* details at the end of this book.

The first and most important thing about credit control is to be sure who owes you money. The second important aspect is to ensure that, once their credit term has expired, you send them a statement to remind them that they now have to make payment. You will find that very many customers will not pay until they are sent a statement, particularly larger companies. To send statements is, therefore, essential.

If the customer does not pay within a reasonable period of time of having been sent a statement, eg a further fifteen days or so, then it would be quite appropriate to send another one. This one should perhaps have a covering letter along the following lines:

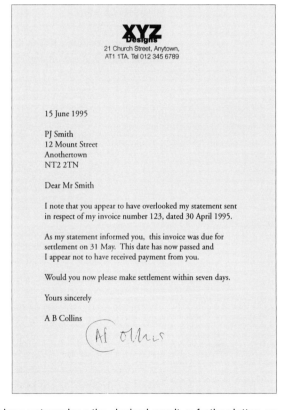

Example of first letter requesting
payment if statement is ignored

If this letter does not produce the desired result, a further letter, as shown on the next page, may be sent. Allow about seven days for postal delays and, if you then have no cheque to show for your efforts you have a choice to make. The first is to give up. On occasions this is appropriate. If you realise you have sold your work to someone who

Final letter before abandoning hope
or taking legal action

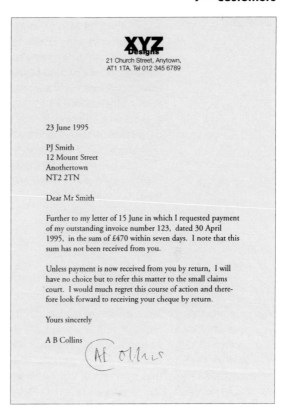

XYZ
Designs
21 Church Street, Anytown,
AT1 1TA. Tel 012 345 6789

23 June 1995

PJ Smith
12 Mount Street
Anothertown
NT2 2TN

Dear Mr Smith

Further to my letter of 15 June in which I requested payment
of my outstanding invoice number 123, dated 30 April
1995, in the sum of £470 within seven days. I note that this
sum has not been received from you.

Unless payment is now received from you by return, I will
have no choice but to refer this matter to the small claims
court. I would much regret this course of action and therefore look forward to receiving your cheque by return.

Yours sincerely

A B Collins

has no intention of paying and who has few assets, then you have very little chance of recovering payment. It may be best to abandon hope of getting paid and not waste further time.

If you believe the person who you have sold the work to could pay but is being awkward, it is worth taking the matter further. If the debt is less than £1000, the most appropriate course of action, having already threatened your customer, is to take out a claim in the small claims section of the county court. You should claim at a county court covering either your workplace, if it was there the contract between you and the customer was agreed, or at the county court covering your customer's location, if you agreed the terms at their premises; ie basically at the court covering the area where the contract was agreed. Unfortunately the court system requires that a claim be filed in the appropriate geographically-located court, and if it is filed in the wrong court the claim will not be valid.

The staff at most county courts are extremely helpful and will assist you in seeking to recover your debt. They will also provide you with useful publications and advise you of the costs. In general terms these should not exceed 10% of the value of the invoice you are trying to recover. Such costs are recoverable from the defendant if you win. If your debt is above £1000, it may be worthwhile seeking the advice of a solicitor before proceeding. Do check that the solicitor deals in debt cases. Also ask for a quote of costs before going ahead or you might be wasting good money chasing a bad debt.

If you feel that taking a county court action in the first instance is rather too severe, many solicitors will write a letter on your behalf for a very modest fee (often only £20, or less) to chase a debt. Few people like receiving solicitors' letters. This action can be as effective as issuing a court summons.

Problems with galleries

For more information on exhibition contracts with galleries, see AN Publication's *NAA Public Exhibition Contract* and *Selling Contracts:* details at the end of this book.

Many artists sell work through galleries. In principle this is not a major problem and benefits both parties. But it is highly advisable that written terms are agreed between the gallery and the artist. Many galleries will have such terms prepared for all artists who sell work through them. If this is the case they have probably sought advice themselves and are unlikely to sell your work on any other terms than those they wish to apply. Review the terms carefully and, if they seem reasonable, accept them. Reasonable terms would include:

- recognition in most cases that the gallery is selling work on your behalf and you therefore retain ownership and copyright.
- an agreement of the period of time during which they will put your work on display to the public.
- the conditions on which you may withdraw work, particularly if you wish to withdraw it early.
- a note about the way that prices are to be agreed between yourself and the gallery for the work in question.
- a note about the percentage the gallery will be allowed to retain from the sale value as their commission.
- an agreement to the time they will take to make payment for work they have sold, and the type of documentation they will supply to notify you of the sale having taken place.

- an agreement that the gallery is allowed to add VAT to any agreed sale price, that they are allowed to add VAT onto their commission charge to you and that, if you are VAT-registered, they will pay to you the amount of VAT to be added onto your net selling price, having allowed for their commission.

- if your work is to be specially advertised, you may have an agreement that you will contribute a set sum towards the gallery's publicity costs, and this may be deducted from sums owing to you as well as commissions payable.

- it is likely that some warranty from you to the gallery will be required to assure that the work is original and your own.

- all good agreements have a termination date, ie an indication as to when they come to an end. The advantage of this to you is that it gives you opportunity to re-negotiate a better agreement next time round.

If the above clauses are included in the gallery's house conditions, then accept them. If not, ask for an agreement including the above to be drafted, quite possibly by yourself, and using simple and straightforward English. Ensure that both the gallery and you sign a copy. Keep yours safe. General problems that arise with galleries are:

- **They do not pay on time.** Chase them immediately to discover the problem. If you have any doubts about their intention to pay withdraw all your work as soon as possible. Remember, if you have a written agreement and they have failed to pay, then they have broken the agreement and you can withdraw your work. The agreement should clearly specify that fact.

- **VAT can be a problem.** Some galleries like a 'self-billing' arrangement for VAT. If this is proposed, and you are VAT-registered, it is strongly recommended that you seek professional advice. If other arrangements are suggested, then in principle they should be as suggested in the chapter 'VAT and the artist'.

see 'Galleries', **8 •**
VAT and the artist,
pages 57-62

Remember, galleries are a sort of customer. If you have reason to doubt them, do not trade with them, because you will be giving them more of your work than you would to just one customer. If you have doubts, try to recover your work. If they do not pay, chase them as recommended in the section 'Debt recovery' above. If that does not work, let all other artists using the gallery know, to protect them as well.

see page 67

Complaints

There is no one in business who has not at some time received a complaint. This does not mean that all businesses make mistakes, just that everybody has awkward customers.

The most important thing to do with a complaint is acknowledge it, as tactfully as possible. Try to determine the real cause of the complaint, which is often not what is initially complained about. If it is due to matters beyond your control, then tactfully explain this, in writing if at all possible, because it is easier to be calm through this medium if the customer is really irate. If the complaint is obviously justified, do everything you can to correct it. Nothing else will restore good relations with the customer.

If you cannot see a real justification for the complaint then, particularly in the case of a commission, refer back to your original terms of reference. Check clearly whether you have complied with the requirements agreed at the outset. If you have, then having those terms of reference will really pay for itself, because you can be clear that what you have done is entirely acceptable and the onus is on the customer to prove otherwise. If you are happy that you are right, hold your ground. Let the customer prove you are wrong. If they cannot, but are just trying to find reason for not paying, then consider the debt recovery process. In this case it might be advisable first of all to seek advice from a solicitor.

Awkward customers frequently pursue complaints even in the face of the fact that they are obviously wrong. With this sort of complainant, there are two decisions to be made. The first is never to do business with them again. The second is how to get the maximum possible out of them by way of payment if it has not already been received. Usually this involves the offer of some degree of discount to pacify them with regards to the extent of the complaint made. Judgement alone can be applied in this case. If they have already paid and you are happy that you have done nothing wrong, the simple answer is to cease communication with them, ignore them altogether and decide to do no further work for them.

Most important of all with regard to complaints is to remember that everyone gets them, you are not alone, and you have no reason to lose your confidence as a consequence of receiving one. Usually it is the customer who is wrong. Your problem is that you usually will not be able to say so.

10 • Suppliers

Obtaining credit

If you purchase materials from one supplier regularly, it may be possible to open a credit account with them. This means that the supplier will send you an invoice, usually after they have supplied you with some materials, but you do not have to pay them until the due date of payment, normally thirty days later (depending on their own specific terms). This saves you having to write out a lot of separate cheques and it helps your cash flow.

To open a credit account, a supplier will almost always require some references. Usually two or three are required including your bank, your accountant and an existing trade supplier. If you do not have one, then it may be possible to either give them the name of you accountant, or the person to whom you pay your rent as a substitute. Some suppliers also check on your personal credit or, if you are a limited company, do a company search.

Once you have an account, you should make sure that you settle on a regular basis and not allow it to build up, otherwise it could affect your credit rating not only with that supplier but with other suppliers in the future.

Documentation

It is important, in order to justify the claim for tax relief on your business expenses, that you obtain an original invoice for all purchases you make. This is essential if you are VAT-registered and are claiming VAT back on the invoice. If an invoice goes missing, perhaps in the post, or you lose it, ask the supplier for a duplicate. If you are VAT-registered, simply having the statement showing the invoice is not adequate. It is important to keep all your invoices in a file, either numbering them as they come in and keeping them in numerical order, or keeping them in alphabetical order.

Where you are accepting delivery of goods from a supplier, such as frames made to order and delivered to your premises, it is important to check the number of frames that you have ordered with those delivered. You must not sign a delivery note for goods that you have not had. If there are any discrepancies, you must telephone the supplier immediately and report what has happened. If you do not do ·this, it is quite likely that the supplier would be able to charge you for the goods even though you have not had them.

Complaining

This applies not just to suppliers, who perhaps have delivered you with materials or, for example, frames which are not of an acceptable standard, but also to complaining to your landlord about poor service.

It is important that you first make sure you are not complaining unnecessarily, and that you are sure of your facts. It is important to make sure that you have given clear and precise instructions as to what you actually require, and that the supplier has no comeback on you personally.

If, for example, some frames are delivered to you which are damaged, you should ring up the supplier immediately and inform them of the damage. You should ask them to explain why this has happened, and whether they were like that when they left the premises or whether it happened in transit, what they propose to do about it, how they are going to collect the frames, how long it is going to take, and confirm with them that you will not be paying until such time as the work is corrected and safely delivered to your premises.

It is important when you are complaining to sound entirely reasonable, and not to lose your cool, which would simply create bad feelings between yourself and the supplier. Although you may be extremely annoyed about something having gone wrong, it is probably better to wait for a few minutes in order to recover your composure and to make it seem not so significant before you pick up the telephone. It might also be helpful to make a list of points to refer to during the telephone conversation.

Once you have complained by telephone, you should then follow the complaint up with a letter reiterating the points that you have made. If nothing happens with regard to your complaint, then it is worthwhile to keep chasing it until something does.

If you want to complain to, say, your landlord about the poor cleaning service in your studio, again it is worth making sure that it is definitely the landlord's responsibility, and then either telephone or write a letter of complaint. The letter should set out exactly what has not happened or has (a list of occasions to back up your argument would be useful), together with what you expect to be done about it. It is important to be firm but not aggressive. If you receive no reply, chase by telephone. If you have had reason to complain, and rectification has not happened, never pay until you are satisfied. If you have already paid, check with a solicitor or the Citizens' Advice Bureau as to your statutory rights. In many cases where you can prove your complaint, you should be able to recover your money, but see page 67 you may have to go to court to do so. See 'Debt recovery', 9 • Customers for details of how to use the small claims court.

11 • Banks

It is an inevitable fact of life that if you are self-employed you will have to have a bank account. Choosing a bank will be one of your early decisions when setting up in self-employment.

Many banks go out of their way to advertise that they help small businesses, and in some cases even try to represent that the success of the business is solely attributable to the bank manager. Unfortunately very few self-employed people would agree. Bank advertising creates an impression that is difficult to support with fact! This criticism applies to all banks, and not one in particular. So do not be swayed by the adverts.

There has been a dramatic change in the way that banks service their small business customers over the last few years. The vast majority of banks have now concentrated their business banking activity on business branches, and if it is likely that you will need to use any of the bank's business services, eg loans, overdrafts, etc, then you will almost certainly need to ensure that your account is at a business centre branch. It may, however, be the case that the bank may require you to have a personal account at one branch and a business account at any branch. If that does not suit your needs, choose another bank which will let you have both your business account and your private account at one branch.

If your business banking requirements are likely to be modest, eg small loans or overdrafts for little more than £3,000 in total, then this may well be possible even if the branch is not a business centre, and may have an advantage in that one person at the branch may know all your affairs.

Because almost all the major banks have changed their way of working in the two years prior to writing this book, and most seem still to be in the habit of making further changes, it is not possible to summarise which bank offers which type of service. The best advice is, therefore, to make enquiries of banks, and of persons of whom you know who are in business and are using bank services, to find out what might suit you best.

Because of changes in the way that banks work, it is unlikely that you will be able to develop a relationship with any one manager in a bank. It is now more important to chose the service you want the bank to supply than the person supplying it, whereas in the past people often chose the bank for a particular branch because of its manage.

One recent trend in banking is telephone banking services. Relatively few of these are available as yet for business purposes. But they are in the course of development and some people, particularly with simple banking needs, find them very useful, partly because of their availability to undertake transactions at any-time of the day or night. If the type of service that you require from a bank is never likely to be difficult, then this is an option well worth investigating, and should enable you to keep all your banking arrangements at one place, if that is what you wish for.

Any bank will usually like to deal with all accounts for one person, because this gives them a fair degree of control over that person's affairs. But for the same reason do consider whether you want to have all your banking arrangements with one bank. There used to be a bonus from loyalty to a bank, but this seems to no longer be the case. It can as a result be worth having your business account with one bank and your private account with another one, so that if you fall out with either you always have a ready-made alternative who knows you and may give you the service you are looking for. In the past, there seemed to be a stigma attached to changing banks. This is no longer the case. Banks now very often offer special deals to get customers. If one is particularly good and attracts you, then have no hestitation in investigating it. Also, always make sure that the bank you are using is offering the best terms that are available. If you see that new customers are getting better terms than you are, then ask for the same to be provided to you.

Borrowing and interest rates

It is very important that you realise from the outset that banks do not like lending money to small businesses. This might not be the impression they give in their advertising, but it is true. Unless you own a house which is not fully mortgaged, or you can find someone to guarantee your borrowings from the bank, it is unlikely that you will be able to borrow much more than £3,000 on an overdraft or general loan facility. To ask for more is likely to lead to a polite refusal unless you can show you have been trading for several years, earned a fairly high level of income and can easily afford to repay the borrowings (which often leads one to question why you would need to have borrowed in tl e first place). Put simply, the attitude of most banks is that they do not lend money if there is any degree of risk. They view small business people, particularly those without very high levels of earnings, as risky borrowers. As such they make sure their own risk is limited by not lending very much. Try by all means, and if you are lucky you might find someone who will break the average overdraft limit, but it will not be by much unless you can offer the guarantees they desire. This attitude has only got worse since the recession and there is no sign of it changing.

Because banks view small businesses as being a high risk, they tend to charge them high rates of interest. Interest rates on bank overdrafts and loans are generally quoted as a percentage above what is called 'base rate'. The base rate is closely linked to the Bank of England official lending rate and is invariably consistent between all banks. If the bank views a small business favourably, it might quote an interest rate of between 2.5% and 3% above base rate. Most likely for a new small business, the rate will be 5% above base rate at least. If they view you as being a high risk borrower they might quote at 7% or more, and in this case it is definitely time to try another bank. Try to borrow at between 3% and 4% at the outset, and accept 5%. Above that, suggest the bank may like to think again.

Bank charges

Even if you run a business bank account in credit, the bank will wish to make charges. All banks now have standard tariffs of charges for business accounts. In general every cheque will cost at least 50p, and every time you pay a cheque into your bank it will probably cost about £1. Direct debits and standing orders also have charges, probably slightly lower than the cheque charge. Make sure you know what these are. This is one area where it is easy to compare banks, because these rates of charges are normally published and readily available.

To reduce bank charges to the lowest possible level, check tariff details with care. Write only as many cheques as are strictly necessary, eg do not pay each invoice to one supplier with a separate cheque but add several together before making payment. Likewise it may be worth waiting to pay cheques into your account in batches, because very often you are charged per single pay-in irrespective of the number of cheques lodged each time.

To overcome this problem many people try to run their businesses through a personal bank account. If you are in credit this is usually quite possible and in general terms, if the bank asks no questions, carry on. But do be warned that banks are increasingly asking self-employed people to change their accounts to business accounts.

Alternatives to banks

Another way of trying to avoid charges is by using a building society cheque account. Some building societies are not legally permitted to offer business banking under their constitution and generally, building societies are not well-equipped to handle business banking. One particular disadvantage of using them is that cheques paid to you tend to take a long time to clear, so if you are operating on tight cash budgets you might find this very frustrating. If you are in credit and receive no complaints about the operation of your account, building societies offer a very good deal, usually paying interest on credit balances.

Other services

One thing to avoid from all banks and building societies is the other services they will try to sell you. Invariably they will try to sell you pensions, life assurance, etc. Usually, the bank or building society will be what is termed a 'tied agent', ie they can only sell you the product of one particular company. This means that by and large you will not get as good a buy as if you went to an independent insurance broker. It also means, particularly with banks, that they make very high profits themselves out of the policies they sell, and these do not tend to be as good a product as those available from insurance companies. This is because banks tend to sell you a bank product, not an insurance company one and, not surprisingly, insurance companies are better at insurance business than banks. If you feel pressurised by the bank into buying any of their products, complain. They have no right to make your account conditional upon buying such product unless you have an overdraft of over about £3000, in which case they might require you to take out a small life insurance and credit protection policy to ensure the bank is repaid if you die. The cost of such a policy should be quite modest, and in this one case only is the bank reasonable in making such obligation of you.

Staying with your bank

Once you have chosen a bank, try to foster a good relationship with it. You never know when you might need money. As a matter of policy, write to the manager at least every six months to let him/her know how things are going. Tell him/her the good news as well as the bad. Bank managers are used to only hearing bad news, because people generally go to them when they need to borrow. If you let a manager know when things are going well, and before a need for borrowing arises, it is often the case that s/he will have a greater respect for you and will be more willing to lend money because s/he know that you have the right attitude towards the bank. S/he also know you will act responsibly, and that will mean that s/he will consider you a lower risk, and will probably charge you less on an overdraft as and when you require it.

Loans

The final use you might make of a bank is to borrow money for a specific purpose, eg to buy a car, equipment etc. Such loans tend to be easier to obtain than overdrafts for the general purpose of a business. The banks might refer you on to their hire purchase or leasing companies. It is quite normal and reasonable if they suggest this. If you are planning to buy equipment using hire purchase, then banks tend to be quite favourable in their rates. All the banks trade under different names from the main name of the company for hire purchase purposes. Barclays' hire purchase department is known as Mercantile Credit, National Westminster calls its hire purchase department Lombard North Central, Lloyds own Black Horse Finance, whilst Midland has a hire purchase company called Griffin Finance. Other hire purchase companies may charge more than these companies. For most artists, hire purchase of assets is much more appropriate than leasing because it provides the artist with flexibility as to when the contract should end. Leasing does not always do so.

Bank loans will tend to be operated on the same basis as bank overdrafts. The rules mentioned above will apply.

12 • Residencies

see AN Publications'
Residencies, details
at the end of
this book.

Residencies have become an increasing feature of work for many artists over the last few years. They generally involve the artist signing a contract with some form of institution, to supply their services over a period of time. Several problems arise with this. The first thing is that without a good contract disputes are quite common. AN Publications provides a contract which can be of benefit in this respect and it is recommended that all artists consider this before entering into a residency.

Because the artist is working under contract with regard to a residency, there can be problems with regard to the ownership of any work that is created during the course of that period, particularly with regard to copyright. This matter is again best dealt with by contractual arrangements and the AN Publication's contract can help in this respect.

Taxation problems also quite often arise with regard to residencies. Whilst some organisations granting residencies are quite happy to consider that the artist is self-employed, and usual arrangements in respect of self-employed tax (and VAT as appropriate) apply, for many institutions, particularly those in the public sector, this can be a problem. If the residency is considered to be a supply of educational services by a publicly-owned authority, then it is exceptionally difficult for that authority to consider the residency to be anything other than being subject to PAYE, ie it is an employment. If there is any doubt in this respect, it is always possible for the artist to ask the authority granting the residency to refer the determination of the status of the contract to the person who is called the 'status officer' in the paying authorities' Inland Revenue tax district. It is a specific responsibility of these tax inspectors to determine whether any contract is in fact one of employment or self-employment, and therefore subject to PAYE tax at source or Schedule D tax laws for the self-employed. Some residency-granting authorities will be quite happy to cooperate in this process, which will require the assistance of the artist in providing full details of their other work. Once these tax inspectors have made their ruling, it is almost always binding. The costs of appeal would not normally be worthwhile.

In the event that a residency is considered to be an employment, there can be a problem with regard to direct costs incurred, eg travel, materials, etc. Because the artist will have significant problems in offsetting these costs against income for taxation purposes, it should be ensured that the person granting the residency guarantees to reimburse these costs. There can be a problem in doing this if the artist is VAT-registered. In this case it is wise to bill the residency authority for the expenses with VAT being added.

In one particular circumstance, being considered to be self-employed and having a residency can actually be worse (at least in cash flow terms) than being treated as being an employee. That is where the residency results in work being undertaken on a building, eg a mural is painted. Then, if the artist is considered to be self-employed, the persons granting the residency may have to deduct tax under the builders' sub-contractors scheme, which means that tax is deducted at 25%, whereas if PAYE is operated then there may be a personal allowance to offset against the income in the first instance. Particular care is therefore required in this respect.

Note that, overall, if all expenses are reimbursed to a person undertaking a residency, and the rate of pay for work is the same irrespective of whether it is an employment or a self-employment, the artist should not be significantly worse off if PAYE is to be operated. Tax will probably be paid sometime. Only National Insurance costs might overall be higher. It is also true that tax deducted under a builders' sub-contractor scheme can be reclaimed offset against other tax liabilities. However, if expenses cannot be charged under an employment contract, and if that is what a residency is deemed to be, then the artist might be significantly worse off in this arrangement and care should therefore be taken before any contract is signed.

13 • Insurance

Essential insurance

For further information on insurance, see AN Publications' Fact Pack, *Insurance*.

Insurance is not something that is usually very high on the artist's list of priorities. But you ignore it at your peril. Two sorts of insurance are obligatory:

Public and employers' liability insurance

Every self-employed person should really have these two types of insurance. This is particularly true if the artist has a studio. In effect these policies, which are usually combined, insure the artist against any risk of an accident arising as a result of their work, eg someone attending their studio, falling over and injuring themselves; or the artist dropping their work whilst hanging it and injuring someone. Note that the work is not insured, just the risk to someone else. If you employ someone, even on a sub-contract basis, it is a legal obligation to have employers' liability insurance. For an artist it is probable that the cost of this policy will be fairly low, maybe under £100 per annum.

Motor insurance

If you drive a car, then third party insurance is essential. Make sure your policy covers the use of your car in the course of your business. Some policies do not, and in this case you could invalidate the policy by driving it on work business.

Insuring artwork and equipment

In addition to the above two types of policy the artist may well want to take out a business risks policy to insure against loss of business equipment due to fire, theft, accident, etc. Such a policy may also be extended to cover work being undertaken, so if this is lost for any of the same reasons the artist is insured against the resulting loss of income and the costs of replacing the work. It would, in most cases, be possible to have such a policy extended to cover work whilst in transit to customers or exhibitions, and to cover the work whilst at galleries etc. Most artists will have some doubt about taking out this insurance because it is expenditure which appears avoidable. But, if disaster strikes, having insurance could be the difference between potential financial destitution and being able to continue as a working artist.

Using a broker

It is strongly recommended that the working artist considers all the above policies. To ensure you get the best buy, arrange your policies through an insurance broker. Make quite sure that the broker understands precisely what you want. If necessary, have a meeting with them to explain your business. If the costs are not what you expected, then check that the broker has obtained an appropriate quotation for you. If you are still not happy, try another broker.

Approaching a particular company direct is unlikely to ensure that you get the cheapest buy. Most companies could sell you a policy of the type you want, but a broker should ensure you get the cheapest policy of that type.

You should not have to pay a broker for those services; the insurance companies will pay them a commission. Do not resent this commission since no insurance company will sell a policy cheaper to the public if it is not sold through a broker; they simply make more profit that way. You are therefore not losing out by using a broker.

Personal insurance

In addition to the above policies, there are three other types of insurance that the artist may wish to consider. These are life assurance, permanent health insurance and pensions.

Life assurance

This comes in two forms. The first is just what it describes, ie a regular premium paid to an insurance company, which will, if the person whose life is insured dies, pay back a set sum. Obviously the bigger the sum that is desired to be paid on death, the bigger the premium. This sort of insurance is often taken out in connection with mortgages on buying a home, or on other big loans, to ensure that if the borrower dies the lender will be repaid. In addition it is appropriate to take out this policy if the person whose life is insured will leave dependants, such as a spouse and children. This is to ensure they will have a lump sum to replace the income of the person who died. If you are single and have no dependents or loans, there is little reason to have life assurance.

However, be aware of the second form of this type of insurance, which is known as the endowment life assurance policy. These can be useful with regard to the repayments of mortgages for buying a house or flat, although they are less popular for this purpose than they used to be. Generally they are sold by insurance brokers as savings policies. This is because if the person whose life is assured is still alive at the end of the policy term, then a lump sum is paid anyway. But the rates of return on this sort of policy are only ever attractive if you can afford to keep up the policy for the full term, which is always a minimum of ten years, that is required to get the tax benefits associated with them. Few artists know their future income sufficiently well to commit themselves to a programme of saving over a ten-year period.

Permanent health insurance

This ensures a person is paid income in the event that they are unable to work because of ill health. Normally these policies do not pay out until the insured person has been unable to work for at least three months. Policies that pay out quicker than this are usually very expensive. It is worth noting that 500,000 people a year are off work through ill health for more than six months in the UK (which is over 1% of the adult population). The policies usually pay out for the remainder of a person's expected working life if the incapacity is permanent. The policy can therefore be seen as an effective 'top-up' on state benefits that would be paid to a person if they were unable to work for reason of ill health. Taking such a policy is entirely down to the individual. The risk may simply be one you are not interested in protecting yourself against. Some people may think it essential.

Pensions

A pension policy is money put aside now, in a particularly favourable saving scheme, so you have an additional income to the state retirement pension when you cease work. In practice, retirement is now allowed at any age from 50 onwards. This form of savings has particularly favourable tax treatment as, subject to age limits, a percentage of a person's income may be paid into a pension policy and these payments are effectively considered to be a trading expense of their business, thereby reducing tax liability. For a person aged under 35 the limit of income they may pay into a policy is 17.5% of their earnings. For a person aged over 60 the limit is 40% of their earnings.

85

Warnings

Particular care needs to be taken with the above three types of insurance policy. There are very many companies selling life assurance, permanent health insurance and pensions. Most people selling the policies earn good commissions on doing so. There is inevitably, therefore, a high degree of selling taking place. All life assurance and pension sales people are now regulated by law, but unfortunately this has yet to prevent misleading advice being given.

Without any doubt the most effective course of action you can take if you wish to acquire any of these policies is to take advice from an independent advisor. Make sure the broker is a member of a proper regulatory body or profession. Do not sign anything until you are quite sure that you can afford the policies and are quite sure you understand the costs and the potential benefits. If you have doubt, do not proceed. If possible, obtain advice from an insurance broker and then check it with an accountant. Even if you have to pay a fee to have the recommendations checked, compared with the amount of money you will probably be paying into any policy this is a tiny cost to ensure that you have received appropriate advice. The most likely suppliers of this type of service to an artist are members of the PIA (Personal Investment Authority), the Law Society, which regulate solicitors with regard to the sale of this type of policy, or an Institute of Chartered Accountants, which does the same for accountants. Always make sure that the advice you obtain is in writing.

14 • Pricing your work

For further information on pricing work, see AN Publications' *Selling:* details at the end of this book

Every artist faces the dilemma of how to price their work. Until your work is so popular that the market itself dictates the price (by which time you could be dead) you will have to live with this difficulty. To come to an initial figure to price your work, calculate how much you need to live. Then work out on a realistic basis how many pieces you can sell a year, whether this be measured in performances, prints, tapestries, or hours worked. Make reasonable allowance for the time that you will have to spend dealing with administration, promotional work, on holiday, and make sure you have excluded from your calculations all time you wish to devote to work which is not intended for commercial sale. When you have an idea of how much work you will be able to produce in this time make sure that the answer is logical, eg few people can reasonably expect to make a living on 200 hours work a year, nor can many actually work more than 1,600 hours a year if all administration time etc has already been excluded.

When you have then come down to a realistic estimate of the quantity of work that will be saleable, calculate how much it will cost you in materials, or other direct costs, to produce this work. Again be realistic. Assume things will go wrong, and make a sensible allowance for this. Make a note of this figure. Then calculate the overheads you are likely to incur in your business. Overheads are such things as rent, telephone costs, accountancy and other advisory costs, stationery and postage costs etc; the costs of research, subscriptions, etc; and any other items that might be appropriate to your particular situation. Travel costs or the costs of running a car normally fall into this category.

Add together the income you require to live on, your overheads and the direct costs you are likely to incur in producing your work, and the result will be the total sales income you need to make in a year. If you divide this by the number of units of work that you consider you can produce and sell, you will have calculated the average selling price for your work. All you then have to do is adjust that selling price for pieces of work that are of greater or lesser extent than the average, always remembering that you have to come back to the average eventually if you are to achieve your financial objectives.

If the resulting price appears impossibly high, re-check your calculations to ensure that they are realistic. If they are, then, if you still consider the result too expensive for the market to bear, you have difficult choices to make. First, see if you can increase the quantity of work that you can make and sell. Remember if you do, your direct costs will increase and you must take this into consideration in your calculations, but since one of the major factors in determining price is the number sold, it is maybe the only choice you have if you want to achieve your financial objectives. If you believe this is not possible, then you have to consider whether you should undertake alternative work to finance your art since, if your work is obviously not saleable at a price sufficient to earn you a living then, unless you have a private source of income, you will not be able to pursue the work for long. This will require long and careful thought.

Of course, you might be pleasantly surprised. The price you work out might be lower than the market is willing to bear for your work. In this case charge more and accept a better level of income than you had anticipated.

This last point is terribly important. Do have the confidence to charge enough for your work. If you really believe it is good, make sure you project that image to the world. If you do, the probability is they will believe it and be willing to pay for it.

The other important point to remember on costing is that you must evaluate your own time. For most artists, this is effectively what they are selling. If you want to make a living as an artist it is therefore important that you dedicate enough of your time to work (which requires discipline), and that you value that time sufficiently. It is a generally acknowledged fact that it is exceptionally difficult for someone to work more than about 1,600 hours a year and be productive. Time is lost to administration, promotion, etc. This reduces the amount of time available. If you want to make £12,000 per year, which no-one would consider a high level of earnings, this means that you must make at least £7.50 an hour from your work, in the assumption that you have no overheads. Most people do, of course, have such costs, and on general terms you should not really consider charging less than £10 per hour for your time. It is important to bear this constraint in mind.

The final and most important aspect of costing that an artist must remember is that materials cost money which must be recovered in the price of the eventual work. In the not totally unrelated area of design work, it is normal for the direct costs of materials included in work to be charged onto customers, with handling charges of at least 15% added on top of their initial price to cover the costs of administration and buying etc. This seems a particularly good guideline for the artist to try to follow as well, ie the price of their work should cover the costs of the materials included in it plus at least 15%, plus the value of time the artist has spent on the work, plus a contribution towards the artist's overheads, if it is to be sold at a sufficient price to ensure that the artist can continue to live on the proceeds.

15 • Artist as employee

see 'Self-employed?', 1 • Turning porfessional, pages 6-12 The difference between self-employment and employment has been outlined in the chapter, 'Turning professional'. The distinction between employment and self-employment is a grey area and in deciding this the Inland Revenue use a long list of criteria in order to make an evaluation. There are however no hard and fast rules, and an individual case can only be decided on the facts and by reference to decided legal cases.

The Inland Revenue uses such things as direction and control, notice period, whether or not you are working exclusively for one person, the number of different engagements, whether you are VAT-registered, whether you take any financial risk, the appearance of your business, eg letterheads, paying studio rent etc, how you were recruited, whether you had specific skills that mean no one else has to tell you how to do your work, what benefits you obtain from the employment such as sick pay, holiday pay, maternity rights, whether you are held out as being connected with your employer, whether you use your own equipment, as well as other criteria, in deciding whether you are or are not an employee. The Inland Revenue look at an overall picture of all the facts relevant to your work in making their decision. For example, if you were working for one person in their studio and had no unusual skills then you would be quite likely to be considered an employee.

A major reason why the Inland Revenue may decide to investigate whether you are employed or self-employed is as a result of an Inland Revenue internal audit of a large company's affairs. For example they may go into a large animation house or design studio and inspect all its records. They may then investigate everyone who works there, and whether or not they have freelance status, to see whether they are to be considered to be an employee of that studio or not. If they rule that freelance people working there are employees, then it will be very difficult to get any tax relief on your expenses against this employment.

Expenses

If it is decided that the work you do for a particular studio is an employment, then the only expenses you can obtain tax relief for are those incurred 'wholly, exclusively and necessarily' for the purpose of your work. It is very difficult to obtain tax relief on almost any expense under this category. The only types of expenses you are likely to be able to recover are expenses not reimbursed by your employer for such things as travel between a studio and a client, payment for couriers, potentially a union or professional subscription, or where you have to provide your own art materials, tools or equipment. The test is very narrow, however, and if you obtain any personal benefit from an expense, or would not lose your job if you did not incur it, then it is not considered to be allowable for tax offset against your employment income.

If you are in this situation then the only way that you can get your legitimate business expenses reimbursed is to make your employer pay them to you by way of an expense claim. This would obviously be something that you and the other artists would have to work out in conjunction with the studio.

Status disputes

Where an Inland Revenue internal audit has indicated that all persons working at a particular studio should be considered to be employees you may want to challenge this by requesting an 'NT' (No Tax) tax code from a tax office. This may involve you in a status dispute and it will certainly involve lengthy negotiations, possibly with two tax offices, about the detail of the work you do, who has control over you, what benefits you have and all the other factors relevant to determining employment or self-employment. If you think that you have a good claim to be considered to be self-employed, it may be possible to get the district dealing with the studio you work for to give you an 'NT' tax code, which means that no tax will be deducted from what you earn and you will then declare your income in your accounts in the usual way.

First of all you should write to your own tax office outlining the facts and supplying a copy of any contract you have, asking them to liaise with the tax office dealing with the studio. You will need to give them the full address and reference number. There is probably in each individual case only a fifty-fifty chance of success here, and if you are only going to be working for the studio for a short time then it is probably not worth your while to do this. You will have to fill out several forms and answer a lot of questions for them to make up their minds. On average it takes up to a year for such a case to be resolved, and only then if quite a lot of pressure is put on the Inland Revenue by way of telephone calls and letters.

If you decide it is not worth trying to claim an 'NT' tax code or arguing about your status, then you will simply accept that you are an employee and obtain all the benefits which go with being an employee such as the right to sick pay, maternity pay, holiday pay, employment protection, etc. The money that you earn will be taxed and this should be disclosed on your tax return as an employment. You will given a form *P60* (certificate of pay and deductions) at the end of each tax year. It is important to keep this since you often cannot obtain a duplicate.

There is only likely to be a complication with your employment which needs disclosing to the Inland Revenue on your tax return where you have an existing self-employment, or you had one within the last year, or where you are paid over £8,500 and receive perks from the employment such as a company car. In this situation the tax which has been deducted from your pay may not be correct and you may owe extra tax. You need advice in this situation.

see 'Expenditure with a dual purpose', **4 •**
Tax problem areas, page 35

16 • Artist as employer

The points noted in the previous chapter about the relationship between employment and self-employment are very relevant to an artist who needs to employ someone or offer sub-contract work.

see pages 90-92

You must decide first whether the person working for you is self-employed or an employee. Refer to the previous chapter, 'Artist as employee', which will help you with this. If you are in any doubt, seek professional advice.

If you are actually employing someone then you should recognise that the person will have certain employment rights such as holiday pay, sick pay, maternity leave, etc. There are detailed rules on these which are beyond the scope of this book, but you may well need to seek professional help with these areas.

It is probably also worthwhile drawing up a contract of employment between you and your employee setting out what their rights are as to notice periods, days of holiday, hours of work, duties to be carried out, etc. Either you can do this yourself or you can have an accountant or solicitor do this for you. A letter is sufficient to constitute such a contract. The Department of Employment can supply you with a separate contract of employment.

PAYE and National Insurance

When you take on an employee you must deduct Pay As You Earn (PAYE) and National Insurance from their salary. You must contact the Inland Revenue to obtain a PAYE scheme. This is best done by contacting your local office and asking which office deals with PAYE matters for your area. It is unlikely to be the same district which deals with your self-employment.

Once you know the district you should telephone them and ask for 'New Schemes Department'. They will then ask you basic questions such as your personal details, the number of employees you will have, etc. They will then send you a PAYE pack.

If you have no previous experience of operating PAYE and National Insurance then you should ask somebody to teach you how to do this – a friend, or your accountant, or failing that the Inland Revenue. It is highly unlikely that you will be able to work out accurately how to operate PAYE from the information sent by the Inland Revenue unless you have some previous idea. There are many detailed rules with regard to PAYE and it is worth having somebody that you can ask about these. If you have no one else to turn to, reading the information in the PAYE pack will obviously be helpful, and then you should telephone the Inland Revenue with any specific queries.

It is important that you operate tax and National Insurance correctly as you go along, otherwise you could be liable to make up any errors at a later stage and these will then have to come out of your own pocket.

Whilst a full description of the PAYE tax scheme is beyond the scope of this book, in outline you will be given a blue deduction card for your employee which will be sent to you in the PAYE pack (form *P11*). This needs to be completed with the monthly or weekly wage, together with the tax deducted and the National Insurance deducted, which leaves net pay. It is in calculating these figures from the tables supplied that you will probably need assistance. There are also columns for recording the employer's National Insurance, which is charged at a maximum of 10.2% on the gross money that you pay your employee. There are also columns for recording the cumulative amount paid to your employee and the cumulative tax deducted from your employee in any given tax year. Once you have calculated this information on the deduction card you should also put the information on a pay slip and give this to your employee together with their monthly or weekly cheque.

At the end of each financial year, ie at 5 April, you will be sent an end-of-year return to complete. This is called a form *P35*. This requires you to summarise the information on the deduction card and gives indication of whether or not the amount of money that you have paid over by way of tax and National Insurance to the Inland Revenue during the course of the tax year agrees with what you should have paid over. You also have to summarise the information onto a form *P14* to send with the form *P35*. The form *P14* is a triplicate set, the last of which is a form *P60* which the employee receives and with which you may be familiar. Every effort must be made to complete forms *P35* and *P14* on time. Penalties and interest can be charged on late submission of the forms. May 19 is the technical deadline but a two-week extension is usually allowed.

As well as your PAYE pack you will be sent a yellow pay slip book and you must use this to pay over the total National Insurance and the PAYE deducted each month to the Inland Revenue. Payment for a month is always due to be paid to the Inland Revenue by the 19 of the following month. Interest is charged on any payments made later than 19 April after the end of the tax year.

There are many detailed rules regarding the completion of forms *P45* for employees starting and leaving, forms for employees earning under the tax or National Insurance limits and for people on different tax codings and if you are employing someone you will probably need to seek professional advice to ensure that you follow these correctly.

Further information

Advisory Concilliation & Arbitration Service, Head Office, 11-12 St. James Square, London SW1Y 4LA or contact your local office

ACAS produces a series of free booklets to help anyone involved in introducing new employers to their workplace. The series covers: *Job evaluation, Payment systems, Personnel records, Labour turnovers, Absence, Recruitment and selection, Induction of new employees, Workplace communications, The company handbook* and *Employing people.*

17 • Keeping accounts

There are numerous bookkeeping methods and no one method is perfect for everyone. The important thing is that you feel happy with your system. Two systems are included in this book – one for those who are non-VAT-registered, which should be suitable for most artists and designers, and one for those who are VAT-registered under the cash accounting system. If you are registered, turn to the chapter see pages 105-133 'Being VAT registered' and 'VAT accounts'. If not, stay with this one.

Who should use this?
Sole traders and freelance people who are not VAT-registered, and who have only a relatively limited number of expenses. Such a person would be likely to work from home or a shared studio and to supply a service rather than a product, for example an artist or designer, photographer, musician, etc. The system in this chapter is not complicated and needs more common sense than mathematical ability.

What is covered?
The chapter covers the maintenance of basic manual accounting records to enable an accountant to prepare simple income and expenditure accounts for agreement by the Inland Revenue.

What you will need:
- an accounts book such as those supplied by any good stationers. The most suitable one is what is called 4 debit, 16 credit. You can record your income on the 4 column side and your expenses on the 16 column side.
- alternatively if you have a computer you can set up a simple spreadsheet to keep the books decribed below.
- 2 ring binder files, A4 paper and staples.
- a calculator.

Sales and income

see 'Sales invoices',
9 • Customer,
page 63

When you send somebody an invoice for work you have undertaken for them you should supply an invoice either by handwriting one in a duplicate or triplicate book (those with carbon paper in between the pages), or by typing or handwriting an invoice on ordinary headed paper.

Income Book

XYZ Designs – Income Book

Date	Ref	Name	£	Date Paid	How Paid
21.6.95	100	Peter Grey	150.00	21.6.95	Cash
28.6.95	101	Imp Magazines	600.00	10.7.95	Bank
30.6.95	102	J Graphics	300.00		
30.6.95	103	Hudson Press	1000.00	1.8.95	Building Society
30.6.95	104	Westmister Council	100.00	30.8.95	Bank
			2150.00		

Income Book recording invoices sent out. Each invoice is marked when paid, showing where the money is paid into.

The invoice should show your name and address, the person to whom you are sending the invoice, their address and the date, and it should be given a reference number if it is not already pre-numbered. The invoice should show the work you have done and how much you are charging for it. You are not VAT-registered so you do not in any circumstances charge VAT.

When you have sent out the invoice to your customer, if you have used a duplicate or triplicate book you will be left with copies of the invoice in the book. If you have written or typed these onto headed paper then you should make sure that you keep a photocopy for your own records. This is most important. You should file these invoices in invoice number order in a ring binder file.

When your customer pays the invoice you should write on the invoice the word 'paid' and the date it was paid.

To write up these invoices you will need to head up the columns in your book. In the first column write the date, in the second column write the invoice reference number, in the third column write the name of the person to whom you are sending the invoice, in the fourth column write the amount of money shown on the invoice and in the final column show the date it was paid and where the money was paid into. For example this might show that it was paid into your current account or if you operate more than one account you could show that it was paid into a building society account. If it was paid in cash you should write 'cash' beside it. Your income book should therefore be a complete record of all sales income.

When you come to the end of a month you should add up the amount of the invoices which you have sent out. You should also check each month that your sales in the last twelve months have not taken you over the VAT registration limit.

It is important that you write up the invoices in invoice number order. If you cancel an invoice for any reason you should still write the invoice number in your book and write "cancelled" beside it.

An example of how to do this is shown on the next page. This system will enable you to see at a glance how much you have made in the way of sales and if you have any invoices outstanding which have not been paid.

When you set up in self-employment you should open a separate bank account for your business. This is described in more detail in the chapter 'Banks'. If you do not do this, but instead use one bank account for both personal and business purposes, it is extremely important that you are able to identify and explain all non sales income amounts paid into the account. This involves extra work in addition to writing up the income book because the income book records sales income only.

You should keep a record of non-sales income paid in, either by using a paying-in-slip book and writing a full description in the book of non-sales income, or by annotating the face of your bank statement, when you receive this each month, for all non-sales items. Examples of this might include birthday money, repayment of a loan to a friend, housing benefit, etc.

If you maintain a separate bank account for your business there should be relatively little non-sales income going through the account, although it is still important that you can explain all non sales receipts as described above and the source of all payments into your personal account.

Expenses and payments

Whenever you pay an expense for the business, you should make sure that you keep the receipt for it. If you are unable to get a receipt, for example for such things as tube fares, magazines or other odd

Expenses Book

XYZ Designs – Expenses Book

Date	Ref	Description	Total £	Travel £	Stationery & Post £	Equipment £	Materials £	Telephone £	Reference Books £	Motor £	Research £	Sundry £	Drawings £	How Paid
1.6.95	1	Tube to Client	2.60	2.60										Cash
1.6.95	2	Envelopes & Stamps	5.00		5.00									Cash
3.6.95	3	Taxi to Client	4.50	4.50										Cash
5.6.95	4	Courier	8.00									8.00		Cheque
10.6.95	5	Petrol	15.00							15.00				Cr Card
10.6.95	6	Smiths Garage	79.00							79.00				Cheque
15.6.95	7	Wheatsheaf Brushes	10.99				10.99							Cheque
16.6.95	8	Dillons Art Book	25.00						25.00					Cr Card
17.6.95	9	C & J Letratype	47.00				47.00							Cheque
17.6.95	10	Answerphone	60.00			60.00								Cr Card
17.6.95	11	A B Art Supplies	22.50				22.50							Cheque
22.6.95	12	Mercury	72.86					72.86						Cheque
25.6.95	13	Exhibition Ticket	3.50								3.50			Cash
26.6.95		Drawings for self	600.00										600.00	Cheque
26.6.95	14	Class 2 NIC	23.00										23.00	D/Debit
26.6.95		Petrol	15.01							15.01				Cheque
30.6.95	15	Tube to Client	2.60	2.60										Cash
			996.56	9.70	5.00	60.00	80.49	72.86	25.00	109.01	3.50	8.00	623.00	

expenses, then buy yourself a pad of petty cash vouchers and simply write down a description of what you have bought, date of purchase and how much it costs. Do be aware, however, that the Inland Revenue can query the inclusion of an expense in your accounts where there is no supporting receipt, and you should therefore get a receipt wherever possible.

Each month you should collect up all your receipts and save them in a safe place such as an envelope labelled with the month and the year. At the end of the month you should write them up in your books.

To do this you will need to head up the columns in your book. You should head up the first column with the date, the second column with a reference number, the third column with the name of the person from whom you have bought the goods or services, or a description of the purchase, and the fourth column with the total amount that you have been charged. For the other columns you should allocate headings that are appropriate for your business. Such headings might include materials purchases, postage and stationery, travel, equipment, advertising, etc. If you refer to the list of expenses in the chapter 'Tax and self-employment', you should head the columns up with the ones that are most appropriate to your business.

You should then number all the receipts which you have and write them up in order number into the books. You should put the total amount in the total column and then repeat the total amount under the appropriate category of the expenditure.

For the first item in the example you will see that the expense is for a tube fare and the amount is £2.60. This goes both in the total column and under the travel column. At the end of each month or any other suitable interval you should total up all the columns. The total of the total column should equal the totals in all the other columns. If you have a computer and set up the expenses book as a spreadsheet you should include a check digit to ensure this works.

When you have written up all the expenses, you should then organise the vouchers so that they can easily be referred to. The best way of doing this is to staple the vouchers on to a sheet of A4 paper in reference number order and then file them in one of the binder files.

Since you are not VAT-registered you do not need to allocate out any VAT on your expenses, and for all purposes VAT should be ignored. You should simply record the total amount you pay for the goods or services.

You should also record all money you take from the business for your use. Do this by recording it as if it were an expense and analysing it in a column called 'drawings'. This would normally include both regular amounts to cover your personal living expenses and also other payments for non-business purposes.

You may also have expenses which are paid directly out of your bank account for which there is no monthly receipt, such as business bank account charges. If this is the case, these expenses should be extracted by checking your bank statement each month and adding these items to the expense book.

It is not necessary under this bookkeeping system to record expenses in separate books depending on the way in which they are paid. You should, however, record whether the expense was paid by cheque (and the cheque number), cash or credit card in the final column on the expenses page.

If you take credit from a supplier you should write the invoice up in the expenses book when it is paid.

If you take any goods from the business for your own use, for example if you are an artist and give a friend one of your paintings as a present, then you must record the value of the painting in your books. You should keep a record on a separate page in your book and make sure your accountant is aware of this when your year end accounts are prepared.

Equipment

Purchases of equipment should be written up in the expense book in their own column and you should always include a description of the equipment purchased.

Equipment which you owned before you started being self-employed can be included. You should not however include it under your expenses, but should make a separate list at the back of your book of the items and their approximate value when you started being self-employed. You should draw your accountant's attention to this list.

see 'Tax deductable expenses', **3 • Tax and self-employment**, page 27

There is a different tax treatment for equipment which is capital expenditure, and this is described in more detail in the chapter 'Tax and self-employment'.

Year-end routine

Under the above bookkeeping method you are writing up your business expenses as you pay them. For most small sole traders who are not VAT-registered, this will be the same date as the expense was incurred because no credit will be taken.

If, however, you are allowed credit by somebody you buy goods or services from, then at your accounts' year-end you may have received purchase invoices which you have not paid and which are therefore not written up in your expenses book.

For purposes of preparing your annual accounts, your accountant will need details of such expenses. Therefore at your year-end date you should make a list of any invoices received from suppliers but not paid, showing the suppliers' name, description of goods or services and total cost. Your accountant will then be able to make an appropriate adjustment in your year-end accounts. You should then write up the expense as normal in your book in the month in which it is paid, and your accountant will make an approriate adjustment after the year-end to ensure it is not included twice in your accounts.

If you have any stocks of goods on hand at your year end you should make a list of all items and show the cost to you of each. The value of stock should be included in your year end accounts. If you have any work in progress at your year end you should discuss this with your accountant to establish a work in progress value.

Your annual income and expenditure account for submission to the Inspector of Taxes will be prepared from your income and expenses books and supporting records. An example of an income and expenditure account is included at the end of this chapter.

Currently businesses with a total annual turnover of less than £15,000 (1995/6) are only required by the Inland Revenue to state total turnover, total business expenses and net profit, commonly referred to as "three-line accounts". These figures can be entered directly onto the tax return form. The Inland Revenue have stated, however, that a tax payer must still keep accurate business records to ensure the correctness of the three line accounts and such accounts can still be subject to investigation and enquiry as to the composition of the expenses.

Therefore you do still need to keep detailed books and records as described in this chapter, even if your turnover is below £15,000.

The Inland Revenue and business records

Under the new self-assessment rules which come into force in 1996/7, the Inland Revenue have ruled that business records needed to make a correct and complete return must be kept by all self-employed persons. Failure to keep such records can result in a penalty being charged of £3000 for each failure.

Your detailed books and records must be kept up to the fifth anniversary of 31 January following the year of assessment. Where, however, a return is subject to enquiry by the Inland Revenue, a sole trader must preserve the records until the enquiries are completed, if later. The same maximum penalty as referred to above, ie £3000, is chargeable for failure to do this. For example, if there was no enquiry into your accounts and you made up your accounts for the year ended 5 April 1999, you would have to keep all those records until 31 January 2005. If you made up your accounts for the year ended 30 April 1999 you would have to keep all your books and records until 31 January 2006.

The books and records you should keep must include your bank statements, cheque stubs and paying-in slips, supporting invoices for expenses, copy sales invoices, your income and expenses books and a year-end stock record if applicable. You should also keep your personal bank or building society statements as the Inland Revenue can require to see these in addition to your business records.

Hints to easier bookkeeping

- Always write a full description, including invoice numbers, any discount taken, the date and the amount paid on all your cheque book stubs.

- Always write who you received money from on your paying-in book, including the bank's copy, whether the receipt is for business or not and whether the account is used for the business or not.

- File or keep all sales invoices in reference number order using the ring binder files mentioned in the introduction. You might like to keep all unpaid sales invoices in a separate file.

- File your small receipts in reference number order (see example page) by stapling or sticking the vouchers to A4 paper and filing.

- You may find, if you use the analysis book to write up your records, that you have far more expenses than you have receipts and the two get out of phase. Do not worry about this, but each year you may like to start writing up the receipts level with your payments again and leave several pages of the receipts blank.

- Keep all your bank statements and make sure you can always easily explain all receipts into all accounts. If necessary write a description on the statement.

Income and expenditure account for the year ended 31 Aug 95

	1995 £	1995 £	1994 £	1994 £
SALES		8,718		7,171
LESS: DIRECT COSTS				
Materials	620		489	
		620		489
GROSS PROFIT		8,098		6,682
LESS: OVERHEADS				
Travel	411		392	
Motor	450		335	
Telephone	83		40	
Stationary & Postage	43		45	
Reference Books	51		68	
Research	75		66	
Sundry	20		16	
Acountancy	270		259	
		1,403		1,221
PROFIT FOR YEAR		6,695		5,461

18 • Being VAT-registered

The basic principle is that, once a person or organisation is registered for VAT, they must charge VAT at the appropriate rate on the goods and services they supply to customers. At present there are three normal rates of VAT: standard rate, zero rate and exempt. Fuel is also charged at a special rate of 8% (1995/6). A brief list of the general categories of zero rate and exempt items is given later on in this chapter.

see 'Zero rated and excempt items', pages 110-111

Charging VAT

Assuming VAT will be charged at the standard rate, then the artist who is registered must, when they prepare their bill, add VAT at the standard rate. In 1995/6 this is 17.5%. This means that if an artist wishes to sell a piece of work and themselves receive £200, they must raise the invoice in this sum and then add VAT at 17.5% to it, ie £35 is charged and the customer pays a total of £235. When the customer pays, the artist can keep the £200 as their own, but the £35 must be paid to Customs & Excise because this is VAT that has been collected on their behalf.

Reclaiming VAT

To compensate the VAT-registered person for acting as an unpaid tax collector, if they are charged VAT by any person for trade goods or services, then that VAT can usually be reclaimed from Customs & Excise on the VAT return. VAT on purchases can be set against your VAT liability for most items, but it can not be claimed on:

see 'VAT Returns', page 108

- entertaining
- non-business items

see 'VAT and cars', page 113

- cars
- items for which you do not have a VAT receipt

• items purchased to enable the VAT registered person to make exempt sales. Because very few artists will be in this position this is not considered further in this book but if you discover that you are making sales of exempt items (see the list later in this chapter) then you should check your VAT position with either Customs & Excise or a suitably qualified accountant.

Business items

You can only reclaim VAT on goods or services which have been bought for the business. For example, VAT is charged on domestic furniture. Just because the artist has been charged with VAT and is registered does not entitle them to reclaim this VAT, unless they can demonstrate that the furniture was used for business purposes. If it was partially used for business purposes, there are grounds for making a partial claim, but this will always be subject to agreement with Customs & Excise.

VAT receipts

Proof must be available that VAT has been paid. The only available evidence is a VAT receipt to support the claim. A VAT receipt has the name of the person who supplied the goods or services, their VAT number, the date, and a description of the goods or services. If the total including VAT is in excess of £100, there should be shown separately on the receipt an analysis of the amount charged split between the net sale amount, the VAT amount, and the gross amount. If this analysis is not shown, the amount of VAT charged can be checked if the receipt has a VAT number. Reference should be made to the list of zero rate and exempt items later in this chapters. If the goods or services supplied do not fit any of the descriptions included there, then VAT at the standard rate should have been charged.

see 'Zero rated and excempt items', pages 109-110

To make a VAT claim on the basis of a receipt, even though the amount of VAT is not specified, multiply the gross value, ie the amount paid including VAT, by 7 and then divide it by 47. For example, if a receipt with a VAT number on it for a total of £94 does not have the VAT separately specified and, having checked the list of zero rate and exempt items, it is apparent that VAT at the standard rate of 17.5% should have been charged on the goods or services, multiply the £94 by 7 and divide by 47. The answer, with the assistance of a calculator, will be found to be £14. £14 is 17.5% of £80, which in this case is the net sum charged. It is not 17.5% of £94. **Never multiply a sum including VAT by 17.5% to find out the amount of VAT.**

Because VAT-registered businesses can reclaim the VAT charged to them by other registered businesses it is normally the case that business prices are quoted net of VAT, ie the price before VAT is added. The non-VAT-registered person must take care to ensure there is clarity on this point, or the actual price paid will be somewhat higher than anticipated. The VAT-registered person must be aware that although this is the true price to them, as they can reclaim the VAT, the cash cost will be higher. This must be taken into account if there is not a lot of money around at the time the proposed purchase is to take place.

VAT returns

see 'Registering', **8 •**
VAT and the artist,
pages 57-58

Once registered for VAT, you will receive a return from Customs & Excise once every three months. This will have on it the name of the artist, their VAT number, and will indicate the VAT quarter that it covers. It has to be completed and returned to Customs & Excise, ie be in their hands, by the last day of the month following the quarter to which the return relates. For instance, if the VAT return covered the quarter 1 June to 31 August, the return must be with Customs & Excise by 30 September. If the return is not submitted on time there are further fines.

When a VAT return is submitted late, the artist should expect to hear from Customs & Excise, who can issue a Default Surcharge Notice notifying the artist that if they submit a further VAT return late within the twelve months following the date on which the late return was due to have been submitted, they will be fined 2% of the VAT owing on the return in question or £30, whichever is the greater. The next VAT return submitted late, if within twelve months of the 2% fine being imposed, will have a 5% fine on it, and the process then continues again until such time as the fines reach 15% of the VAT owing on a VAT return, at which point in time the business is probably being financially crippled by the fine, so they do not increase further. Submitting all returns on time for twelve months always clears the process and all fines then stop. Fines are usually waived if they amount to less than £200.

It is possible to try to defend the imposition of such a fine by providing what Customs & Excise term a 'reasonable excuse'. Reasonable excuses are in fact extremely hard to find by Customs & Excise definition. For the sake of clarity it is emphasised that failure to complete the VAT return because of pressure of work, failure to pay the VAT owing to Customs & Excise with the VAT return because of shortage of funds, or because you were not sent a return, or because you were on holiday, or (in extreme circumstances) failure of the Post

Office to deliver the return unless you can prove that you posted it by having obtained a certificate of postage, are all unacceptable excuses.

It is also the case that Customs & Excise deem a VAT return to be late if it includes an error (eg it has not been signed, or it does not add up), and they have to return the VAT return to the artist for them to correct the error and resubmit it, and the resubmission occurs after the deadline.

VAT Control visits

All VAT-registered persons occasionally have a visit from Customs & Excise so they can check that the VAT returns being submitted are correct. On average an artist would expect to have such a visit once every four or five years. Most people find such visits stressful and it is unfortunate that Customs & Excise do little to relieve such pressure. During the course of a visit of this sort Customs & Excise will normally check at least one VAT return in great detail. The particular points they will be seeking to check are that:

- sales invoices of the business are correctly prepared with the appropriate rate of VAT being shown on them;
- if the business is operating under the cash accounting scheme, as would normally be the case for an artist, and that all receipts of money into the bank are adequately explained, with VAT being accounted for on the receipts;
- there are proper VAT invoices received from suppliers for all VAT claims made from Customs & Excise;
- VAT has only been reclaimed on expenses incurred for the business, or where it is allowable (see the VAT cash accounting book-keeping section for further elaboration);
- books and records that the artist keeps are sufficient to enable a proper VAT return to be prepared;
- the books and records are actually reflected in the VAT returns submitted.

It must be emphasised that Customs & Excise will always be looking for errors in their favour, not yours, will sometimes offer advice which is inappropriate, and some use 'aggressive interview techniques' whereby they will try to ask leading questions that could give rise to confusion in your mind or hasty answers. If you have any doubt at all about a question that Customs & Excise ask, then the appropriate answer is, 'I do not know at the moment. Please put your question in writing and I will then deal with it.' More problems arise between a

VAT-registered person and Customs & Excise as a result of hasty answers given during the course of VAT inspections than for any other reason. Please be careful. If in doubt, say nothing. Unlike the police, Customs & Excise do not have to caution you before being able to use anything you say in evidence against you if a dispute were to reach a VAT tribunal, which effectively is a form of court.

VAT problems

There are some pitfalls of VAT which are always worth avoiding. The most common are:

- charging VAT at the wrong rate to your customers. Almost invariably an artist should charge at 17.5%. Always be wary about charging 0%. This will usually only be for an export (see section on exports).
- filling in the VAT return incorrectly from the books and records. If you want to do this yourself, it is still often advisable to have instruction in the first instance from an accountant to ensure that you are doing it correctly.
- claiming back the VAT from Customs & Excise through your accounts books when this is not allowed.

Note that you are not allowed to claim VAT in the following circumstances:

- you do not have an invoice for the money spent or have a receipt which has not got a VAT number on it, unless the purchase in question is for car parking or for a telephone box call and is for less than £25 in total.
- the expenditure is on entertaining or gifts, even if VAT is charged.
- the expenditure is on the purchase of a car, even if VAT is charged.
- the purchase is not for the benefit of your business, ie you have a VAT receipt for expenditure which is not of a business nature.
- fines, eg car clamping or tow-away charges.

Zero rated and exempt items

The items you are most likely to come across which are zero-rated or exempt are:

109

Zero rated (0%)
- food (excluding sweets and alcohol)
- books and magazines
- train, bus and tube fairs, air flights and ferry crossings
- some exports
- water rates
- new construction work and the sale of new houses by builders.

Exempt (not liable to VAT)
- insurance
- postage, when sold by the Post Office and its agents
- finance charges, bank charges and interest.

But be warned that these are only general guidelines. Customs & Excise publish full definitions which are lengthy in extent and they are noted for being pernickety in the extreme with regard to interpretation and enforcement. If there is any doubt about any category and appropriate rate of tax, contact Customs & Excise themselves to ensure the appropriate charge is made.

Exports

The Government has claimed that one advantage of the '1992' changes introduced by the European Union is easier international trade between the member states. It must be stated that very few businesses are really convinced, and since VAT is a European tax it has got more complicated as a consequence of these changes, rather than easier.

Before the 1992 changes, if an artist could prove that they had exported their goods or services from the UK, then they could usually charge 0% VAT on them. Be warned that this simple life has gone. The rules with regard to exports now require the artists to decide whether:

- they are exporting goods or services.
- whether they are exporting to a person inside or outside the European Union.
- if they are exporting to a person inside the European Union, whether that person is in business or not by way of being able to supply them with their VAT registration number or not.

Most artists will export goods which have a physical existence, ie their work. If this is the case, then what is critical upon export is to obtain documentation that proves goods have been exported, ie a certificate of postage or a bill of lading from a shipping company that proves that the goods have left the UK.

If the artist is exporting their services, eg they are undertaking a residence outside the UK and are registered for VAT in the UK, then they have to obtain very clear proof which they must be able to retain to prove that they did genuinely provide their services outside the UK or its terriotrial waters before they can consider not charging VAT. The customer, if in the EU, must be VAT-registered, and the artist making the sale must be able to prove it, before zero rating can take place in this case. Be aware that this situation initially creates quite a number of VAT problems, not least technically because a supply made in these circumstance is not VAT zero-rated but is outside the scope of UK VAT. Specialist advice is likely to be required on the preparation of appropriate documentation. Customs & Excise provides assistance, or a suitable qualified accountant should be able to give you help.

If the export of goods or services is to someone outside the European Union, then VAT will not need to be charged on the export so long as you can prove there really is an export.

If the export of goods or services is inside the European Union, then whether VAT is charged depends upon whether the purchaser can provide the artist with their VAT number. If they can provide a valid VAT number, then the supply can be zero rated or considered outside the scope of VAT. To check that the VAT number is valid you can telephone Customs & Excise and ask for their assistance in the checking process, and this is strongly recommended. To claim the VAT zero rating, the customer's VAT number must be shown on all invoices and all shipment documents for goods. If a valid VAT number cannot be obtained from a person in the European Union, then despite the fact that the goods are exported from the UK, they must have UK VAT charged upon them.

Any person who makes exports of goods (but not services) from the UK to a VAT-registered business in the European Union must prepare a quarterly VAT European sales listing for submission to Customs & Excise. This is always submitted for calendar quarters ie for the period to 31 March, 30 June, etc and must be submitted within six weeks of the period. The return must include details of value of the goods sold, and the VAT registration number of the purchaser. If the total level of export sales per annum is quite low, application can be made to Customs & Excise to submit this form once a year. As with all forms there are penalties for late submission and incorrect completion, and therefore great care should be taken with regard to the declaration of export sales. It is also the case that if a VAT number has been incorrectly recorded for the person to whom the goods are exported, then Customs & Excise can ask for the VAT to be paid to them by the artist. As a result it is very important that care with regard to VAT numbers is taken.

Mistakes

If any mistakes are found it is essential they are not simply 'fudged' into the VAT return of the period in which they are found, but are separately noted and identified. Mistakes found in a period exceeding £2000, either in the favour of Customs & Excise or of the artist, must be notified separately to Customs & Excise on a form *VAT 652*. If such mistakes are not separately notified, then Customs & Excise have the right to charge a penalty on non-disclosure of these mistakes of up to 15% of their value, if the non-disclosure was in their favour, and to charge interest on the late payment of VAT as a result of the error. On voluntary disclosure of the mistake only interest can be charged, and not the fine. If mistakes less than £2000 are corrected in the period after they are made, there are usually no penalties or interest charges. Persistent errors can give rise to bigger penalties.

VAT and cars

One final problem with VAT is when a registered person owns a car. In the first instance, no VAT can be reclaimed upon the purchase of a car. Likewise, no VAT is chargeable upon the sale of a car unless it is sold for more than it was originally bought for. In this rare circumstance VAT must be accounted for the difference between the purchase price and the selling price.

However, the biggest problem with regard to VAT and cars is that Customs & Excise takes the view that if a self-employed person, or limited company, buys petrol and puts it in a car which is also used for private purposes, then the self-employed person or limited company sells that petrol on to the private user of the petrol even if the self-employed person and the private driver are one and the same person! Rather than try to work out the value of this sale, Customs & Excise have deemed it to have a set value and the latest information with regard to this value will be found in the blue *VAT guide* supplied to all VAT registered persons by Customs & Excise. This charge only has to be made if VAT on the purchase of petrol is reclaimed from Customs & Excise. For very many persons it is the case that more VAT is payable to Customs & Excise than can be reclaimed on the purchase of petrol and as a result it is now quite common for people to decide not to reclaim VAT on the purchase of petrol and so avoid having to pay the liability over to Customs & Excise by way of additional charge. Full clarification of this scheme is available in Customs & Excise's *VAT guide* and on this, as with many other detailed matters, you are encouraged to refer to this guide in the first instance if in doubt.

19 • VAT accounts

Who should use this chapter?

VAT under the 'normal' system: If you are VAT registered but not under the cash accounting system then in addition to the records mentioned under the cash accounting system you will also need to keep a purchase invoice listing, recording your suppliers invoice in date order. You should analyse the VAT in this record and not in the payments cash book. When you prepare your VAT Return you will use the VAT figures from the sales listing, purchase invoice listing and petty cash book.

The accounting method described in this chapter is for sole traders, partnerships and other non-incorporated businesses who are VAT-registered under the cash accounting system. If you operate as a limited company you should refer to your accountant before using this chapter, as it doesn't cover methods of taking money out of a company in respect of services performed by you as a director. If you are VAT-registered, but not under the cash accounting system, you can adapt this method as described in the section below. If you are in doubt about the correct system to use for your business, then there is no substitute for seeking professional advice. You should also read the previous chapter, 'Keeping accounts', as this contains some information which is also relevant to VAT registered businesses, particularly the section on 'The Inland Revenue and business records'.

VAT under the 'normal' system

If you are VAT-registered, but not under the cash accounting scheme, then in addition to the records mentioned under the cash accounting system you will need to keep a purchase invoice listing recording your suppliers' invoices in date order. You should analyse the VAT in this record, and not in the payments cash book. When you prepare your VAT return you will use the VAT figures from the sales listing, purchase invoice listing and petty cash book. It is assumed you will not be using this system in the rest of this chapter.

What is covered?

This chapter covers the layout and maintenance of manual accounting records to help preparation of VAT returns under the VAT cash accounting scheme, and to assist in the preparation of annual accounts. It does not cover computerised accounting systems.

There are a large variety of computerised accounting packages on the market, some of which are aimed specifically at small businesses. If you require a fully-computerised system you should take advice from your accountant or other specialist as to what is suitable for you. Some systems which claim to be aimed at 'small' businesses may have very different interpretations of what constitutes 'small'.

What will you need?
An accounts book such as those supplied by any good stationers. The most suitable one is what is called 4 debit, 16 credit. Alternatively if you have a computer, you can set up simple spreadsheets to keep all the books decribed below.

Cash accounting

Under this scheme a taxable person accounts for VAT according to when payment is made and received, rather than on invoices received and issued.

The cash accounting scheme is designed to help small businesses. The main advantage of it is automatic bad debt relief, because if you never receive money for work done, then you never have to pay the VAT on your sales invoice. The other advantage is the deferral of the time for payment of output VAT where extended credit is given, ie where your customers take a long time to pay you.

This scheme does not tend to be beneficial for businesses which claim net refunds of VAT at the end of the VAT quarter or where the majority of sales are for cash. Similarly, if you take extended credit before paying your suppliers, then the scheme may not be advantageous because you cannot claim input VAT until you have actually made payment to your suppliers.

Admission to scheme
There are detailed conditions to be admitted into the cash accounting scheme and, as long as these are kept, no formal application is required to join the scheme. As a general rule you will be eligible if you estimate that the value of your taxable supplies (excluding VAT) in the next year, from the date of application, will not exceed £350,000. Taxable supplies will almost always include re-charged expenses. For the detailed rules in respect of the cash accounting scheme (and if you are changing over from the 'normal' scheme) you should refer to your accountant or the *VAT guide*.

Exit from the scheme

If your business expands rapidly, then you must leave the scheme if your taxable supplies in any year ending at the end of a prescribed accounting period exceed £437,500 and the value of taxable supplies in the next year exceed £350,000. You must then leave the scheme at the end of the second year. You should refer to your accountant or the *VAT guide* for full details.

Exceptions to the scheme

Hire purchase, conditional sale and credit sale agreements cannot be dealt with under the scheme. You should refer to your accountant or the VAT guide if this is relevant to you. Conditional and credit sales are where the price is payable by instalments, ie similar to hire purchase. If you export goods and cannot obtain proof of export, you should refer to your accountant or local VAT office, as special rules apply.

Operation of scheme

You are liable for output VAT on your sales on the date you actually receive payment of your sales invoice, not on the date you raise the sales invoice to your customer. Similarly, you can claim relief for input VAT on purchase invoices only on the date you pay, not on the date the purchase invoice was raised. This means that the dates on which you receive cash and pay out cash form the basis of your VAT accounting. Therefore the receipts cash book, the payments cash book and the petty cash book are the most important books for the VAT cash accounting scheme. However, it is still necessary to maintain a sales day book or sales invoice listing for accounts purposes. The books you need to maintain are therefore:

• sales day book

• receipts cash book

• analysed payments cash book

• petty cash book.

Sales day book

This should contain a list of all invoices raised to customers in invoice number order.

Writing up a sales day book

• Write the date that you raised the invoice in the first column.

Sales Day Book

XYZ Designs – Sales Day Book

Date	Ref	Name	NET £	VAT £	GROSS £	Date Paid
4.5.95	196	Baytree Systems	3500.00	612.50	4112.50	1.6.95
15.5.95	197	A B Magazines	1500.00	262.50	1762.50	16.6.95
17.5.95	198	R Hall	500.00	87.50	587.50	5.6.95
26.5.95	199	I T Design Co	1150.00	201.25	1351.25	27.6.95
			6650.00	1163.75	7813.75	
1.6.95	200	A B Magazines	1900.00	332.50	2232.50	7.7.95
9.6.95	201	S Software	800.00	140.00	940.00	14.6.95
9.6.95	202	J Graphics	300.00	52.50	352.50	24.7.95
22.6.95	203	Book Press	2900.00	507.50	3407.50	
30.6.95	204	Mega Records	875.00	153.13	1028.13	3.8.95
30.6.95	205	IBP Magazines	1500.00	262.50	1762.50	30.7.95
			8275.00	1448.13	9723.13	
4.7.95	206	S Software	3000.00	525.00	3525.00	4.8.95
10.7.95	207	R Hall	650.00	113.75	763.75	4.8.95
19.7.95	208	I T Design Co	2300.00	402.50	2702.50	
28.7.95	209	A B Magazines	1700.00	297.50	1997.50	28.8.95
			7650.00	1338.75	8988.75	
2.8.95	210	J Graphics	500.00	87.50	587.50	16.8.95
3.8.95	211	N Bates	800.00	140.00	940.00	20.8.95
7.8.95	212	Baytree Systems	3500.00	612.50	4112.50	
14.8.95	213	Mega Records	1200.00	210.00	1410.00	
23.8.95	214	A B Magazines	2000.00	350.00	2350.00	
			8000.00	1400.00	9400.00	

- Write the reference on the invoice in the second column. All invoices should have a reference. These should be consecutive. If for any reason you duplicate an invoice number, call the invoices 101 and 101a, for example. If you miss out an invoice number write it in the book with 'cancelled' beside it.
- Write a description of the person the invoice is raised to.
- Head up the next three columns 'net', 'VAT' and 'gross'.

- In the 'net' column write the value of the invoice before VAT. The net value should include any expenses which are being recharged.
- In the 'VAT' column write the amount of VAT charged on the invoice. This is 17.5% of the net value unless the supply is zero-rated or exempt.
- In the 'gross' column write the total value of the invoice, that is the net value plus VAT. The VAT should equal 7/47ths or 17.5% of the gross value in most circumstances.
- Set up a 'paid' column. When you receive money for a sales invoice tick the invoice, as paid and write the date you received the money beside it.
- Finally rule off the month's invoices and add up all the columns. The total in the gross column should equal the total in the net column plus the total in the VAT column.

Information which you can use from the sales day book listing is:

- you can see debts outstanding at a given date. All items not marked with a payment date are your debtors.
- total sales for the quarter/month can be arrived at by adding up the 'net' column for the quarter/month in question.

If you give a customer a discount on an invoice, you must mark in the sales day book against the date paid column that a discount was given, and the amount. It helps if this is done in red ink.

The sales day book is for accounts purposes only. The total VAT shown in the sales day book is not the amount of VAT which goes on to your VAT return at the end of a VAT quarter. It is very important to remember this.

Receipts cash book

This contains details of all money you receive into your business bank account, whether they are sales, personal money, sundry receipts or bounced cheques. You will take the information to complete the receipts cash book both from your paying-in book and your bank statement. The receipts cash book will also show the VAT element charged on all sales invoices. You will take this information from the sales invoices themselves, or the sales day book. The information

Receipts Cash Book

XYZ Designs – Receipts Cash Book

Date	Name	Sales £	Other £	Total £	VAT Memorandum £	Sales Ref
1.6.95	Baytree Systems	4112.50		4112.50	612.50	196
5.6.95	R Hall	587.50		587.50	87.50	198
14.6.95	S Software	940.00		940.00	140.00	201
16.6.95	A B Magazines	1762.50		1762.50	262.50	197
27.6.95	I T Design	1351.25		1351.25	201.25	199
		8753.75	0.00	8753.75	1303.75	
7.7.95	A B Magazines	2232.50		2232.50	332.50	200
10.7.95	Insurance Claim		220.00	220.00		
24.7.95	J Graphics	352.50		352.50	52.50	202
30.7.95	IBP Magazines	1762.50		1762.50	262.50	205
31.7.95	Bank Interest		10.11	10.11		
		4347.50	230.11	4577.61	647.50	
3.8.95	Mega Records	1028.13		1028.13	153.13	204
4.8.95	S Software	3525.00		3525.00	525.00	206
4.8.95	R Hall	763.75		763.75	113.75	207
16.8.95	J Graphics	587.50		587.50	87.50	210
20.8.95	N Bates	940.00		940.00	140.00	211
28.8.95	A B Magazines	1997.50		1997.50	297.50	209
		8841.88	0.00	8841.88	1316.88	

should be entered in order according to your paying-in book, with additional entries arising from your bank statement being entered at the end of each month.

Writing up a receipts cash book

• In the first column write the date that you receive the money.

• In the second column write the name of the person who paid you the money.

• Head up three columns entitled 'sales', 'other' and 'total'. Analyse the receipts between those received for sales invoices and those which are other receipts. The total column should be used for the total value of each bank paying in slip.

- Head up a column entitled 'VAT memorandum'. Enter here the VAT element of cash received relating to sales invoices. To do this you will have to refer back to the sales day book or sales invoice, so that when you receive payment you can agree the total received to the gross column in the sales day book and correctly write up the VAT memorandum column from the VAT column in the sales day book. You should find that, where you have entered a receipt in the 'other' column, there is no corresponding entry in the VAT memorandum column, because this relates to non-sales cash received into the business such as capital introduced. If you receive part-payment of an invoice you must show the relevant VAT amount in the memorandum column. This can be calculated by taking 7/47 or 17.5% of the gross receipt.
- Write the sales invoice reference number next to the appropriate sales receipt.
- Enter any receipts paid directly into your bank account from your bank statement at the end of each month, for example bank interest received or a BACS transfer.
- Rule off the month's sales receipts and add up the columns. Sales receipts plus other receipts should equal total receipts. The total of the VAT memorandum column should usually be equivalent to 7/47 or 17.5% of the total sales column, unless you make some zero rated or exempt sales in the period.
- When you receive your bank statements, check them against your receipts cash book. If any receipts have yet to clear through the bank at the month-end, ie you have written them in your book but they are not yet on the bank statement, write 'outstanding' against them in your book and remember to make sure that they are on the next bank statement.
- The receipts cash book is normally written up from your paying-in slips. So it is very important that when you pay money into the bank, especially when you make several sales to the same customer, that you note the name of the customer and, if possible, the original sales invoice number on the paying in slip. It is important in your dealings with Customs & Excise and the Inland Revenue that you can identify where all money paid into your bank account has come from.
- The output VAT due for the quarter is arrived at by adding the total of the VAT memorandum column for the appropriate months.

In the example of XYZ Designs VAT due is £1303.75 + £647.50 + £1316.88 = £3268.13

The procedure explained above assumes you will bank all your receipts. It is recommended that you do, but if for any reason you cannot then you should keep two receipts books, one for money that is banked and another for money that is not banked.

Payments cash book

This contains details of all payments from your business bank account whether payments to suppliers, drawings, bank charges or bounced cheques. You will take the information to complete the payments cash book from both your cheque book and your bank statement.

The payments cash book will also show VAT on all payments where this has been charged to you by the supplier. Details of the VAT should be taken from the supplier invoice as it is written up in the payments cash book, and filed in the paid invoices file. The information in the payments cash book should be entered in the order of your cheque book, with additional entries arising from your bank statements being entered at the end of each month.

Writing up a payments cash book

- In the first column write the date the money was paid out.
- In the second column write the name of the person who was paid.
- The next column records the cheque number. The payments cash book should be written up in cheque number order from your cheque book. Direct debits, standing orders and bank charges should be entered into the payments cash book from your bank statements at the end of the relevant month after all the cheques have been entered.
- The next column refers to the reference number of the bank payment. Where you have a supporting invoice in respect of a bank payment, you should reference these consecutively according to the date on which they are paid.
- The next column is used as a 'total' column. This records the amount that the cheque was drawn for and will correspond with the amount.

Analysed Payments Cash Book

XYZ Designs – Analysed Payments Cash Book

Date	Name	Cheque No	Ref	Total £	VAT £	Typesetting £	Materials £	Stationery & Post £	Phone £	Rent £	Courier £	Equipment £	Sundry £	Drawings £
1.6.95	J Studio	710300	299	822.50	122.50					700.00				
2.6.95	Typesetters	710301	300	558.13	83.13	475.00								
5.6.95	Art Supply	710302	301	68.97	10.27		58.70							
10.6.95	B Graphics	710303	302	259.68	38.68		221.00							
13.6.95	Rymans	710304	303	66.42	9.89			56.53						
17.6.95	Typesetters	710305	304	763.75	113.75	650.00								
22.6.95	Art Supply	710306	305	378.35	56.35		322.00							
23.6.95	Fleet Bikes	710307	306	29.63	4.41						25.22			
27.6.95	Dixons	710308	307	587.50	87.50							500.00		
28.6.95	Drawings	710309		1500.00										1500.00
				5034.93	526.48	1125.00	601.70	56.53	0.00	700.00	25.22	500.00	0.00	1500.00
1.7.95	J Studio	710310	308	822.50	122.50					700.00				
3.7.95	British Telecom	710311	309	141.00	21.00				120.00					
10.7.95	Typesetters	710312	310	1034.00	154.00	880.00								
14.7.95	Fleet Bikes	710313	311	37.60	5.60						32.00			
16.7.95	W H Smiths	710314	312	51.70	7.70			44.00						
18.7.95	Stores	710315	313	19.41	2.89								16.52	
22.7.95	Art Supply	710316	314	484.10	72.10		412.00							
28.7.95	Drawings	710317		1500.00										1500.00
29.7.95	National Insurance	D/Debit		23.00										23.00
				4113.31	385.79	880.00	412.00	44.00	120.00	700.00	32.00	0.00	16.52	1523.00
1.8.95	J Studio	710318	315	822.50	122.50					700.00				
4.8.95	Ikea	710319	316	102.18	15.22							86.96		
14.8.95	Typesetters	710320	317	1034.00	154.00	880.00								
20.8.95	Fleet Bikes	710321	318	24.68	3.68						21.00			
20.8.95	Art Supply	710322	319	434.75	64.75		370.00							
28.8.95	Rymans	710323	320	33.84	5.04			28.80						
28.8.95	Drawings	710324		1500.00										1500.00
28.8.95	National Insurance	D/Debit		28.75										28.75
				3980.70	365.19	880.00	370.00	28.80	0.00	700.00	21.00	86.96	0.00	1528.75

- The next column is the VAT column. In this column should be entered the VAT shown as due on the purchase invoice which is being paid. If payment relates to an item on which there is no VAT charged, then the column should be left blank. You must not claim back VAT unless you have a proper invoice showing a VAT number etc. For a detailed list of what should show on a VAT invoice, see the chapter 'Customers'. Small invoices from retailers do not have to show your name and address or separate the VAT element of the purchase. If there is a VAT number on the invoice but the VAT has not been calculated you can do this by taking 7/47ths or 17.5% of the total value of the invoice as long as it is for the purchase of something which is VAT standard-rated.

- You should then analyse your expenditure using as many columns as you need for your business. The figures in these columns will be net of VAT, ie before VAT is added.

- There will be several types of payment for which VAT is not applicable, such as salaries, drawings, bank charges, etc.

- Non-cheque payments should be written up direct from the bank statement once this is received.

- Rule off the month's payments and add up all the columns. The total of all the analysis columns together with the VAT column should add up to the total column.

- When you receive your bank statement you should also agree the cheque payments as per your cash book against the bank statements. Mark any payments which have yet to clear through the bank at the end of the month as outstanding and remember to make sure that they are on the next bank statement.

- The total of the VAT column for the month is the input VAT which can be claimed on the relevant quarter's VAT return.

> For XYZ Designs the Input VAT which can be claimed for the Analysed Cash Payments Book is £526.48 + £385.79 + £365.19 = £1277.46

The information you will not obtain from the analysed cash payments book is details of your liabilities outstanding at a given date. This is because you are writing up your invoices as they are paid, not as the liability is incurred. Therefore you should always maintain two separate files of purchase invoices, one being the unpaid purchase invoices and the other being paid purchase invoices. It is only when you pay the purchase invoices that you should give them a reference number and write them up in the analysed cash payments book. The total value of all purchase invoices in the unpaid invoices file is the value of your outstanding liabilities at any one time.

Accounts year-end

At your accounts year-end you need to determine the outstanding liabilities of the business, ie expenses incurred which have not yet been paid. You must make a complete list of the invoices in the unpaid invoices file, showing the net invoice value, name of supplier and description of what the invoice relates to if this is not obvious from the supplier name. This will enable your accountant to include all your liabilities in the accounts. Depending on the number of unpaid invoices at your year-end, it may be easier to photocopy the whole of the unpaid invoices file. This action must be taken on your year-end date. It cannot be done in retrospect.

Petty cash book

This contains all the items paid for by cash, or cheque from your personal bank account (where you maintain both personal and business bank accounts), or by a credit card, whether business or personal. These will usually be small items and you should have a receipt. VAT should be analysed if it has been charged to you as per the petty cash receipt.

Writing up a petty cash book

- In the first column you write the date that the transaction took place.
- In the next column you should write a description of the item.
- You should allocate to each item a separate consecutive reference number. This should be written on the receipt and also in the third column.
- The next column is the total column. The total cost should be entered here.
- The next column analyses the VAT. If there is no VAT deductible on the petty cash expense, the VAT column should be left blank.
- The net expense should then be analysed between the remaining columns as appropriate for your business.
- Finally, rule off the month and add up the columns. The total of the total column should equal the total of the VAT column plus the totals of the analysis columns.

Petty Cash Book

Date	Description	Ref	Total £	VAT £	Stationery & Post £	Equipment £	Motor £	Materials £	Photocopy £	Ref Books & Mags £	Sundry £	Travel £
1.6.95	Taxi Fare	19	3.00									3.00
5.6.95	Stamps	20	18.00		18.00							
10.6.95	W H Smith - Envelopes	21	3.50	0.52	2.98							
10.6.95	Kalkwick Photocopies	22	10.40	1.54					8.86			
17.6.95	Magazine	23	2.20							2.20		
18.6.95	Tube Tickets	24	4.10									4.10
24.6.95	Tea & Coffee for Clients	25	5.25								5.25	
25.6.95	Tube Tickets	26	4.10									4.10
29.6.95	C J Graphics	27	8.00	1.19				6.81				
			58.55	3.25	20.98	0.00	0.00	6.81	8.86	2.20	5.25	11.20
2.7.95	J Jones - Subcontract	28	50.00								50.00	
6.7.95	Rail Fare	29	11.50									11.50
7.7.95	R T Prints	30	8.00	1.19					6.81			
14.7.95	Rymans Pens	31	6.95	1.04				5.91				
21.7.95	Tube Fares	32	6.80									6.80
23.7.95	Petrol	33	16.90				16.90					
24.7.95	Postage	34	4.50		4.50							
25.7.95	Copies	35	6.80	1.01					5.79			
28.7.95	W H Smiths - Files	36	2.69	0.40	2.29							
28.7.95	ABC Garage - Petrol	37	10.00				10.00					
			124.14	3.64	6.79	0.00	26.90	5.91	12.60	0.00	50.00	18.30
3.8.95	Halfords - Wiper Blades	38	5.99	0.89			5.10					
3.8.95	Colyer Graphics	39	8.99	1.34				7.65				
6.8.95	Magazines	40	3.60							3.60		
10.8.95	Taxi	41	8.00									8.00
11.8.95	Boots Studio	42	1.80	0.27		1.53						
15.8.95	Wheatsheaf Graphics	43	10.70	1.59				9.11				
18.8.95	PB Books	44	8.50							8.50		
21.8.95	Ikea - Shelves for Studio	45	85.00	12.66		72.34						
22.8.95	Locksmith - Studio Keys	46	25.00	3.72							21.28	
27.8.95	Petrol	47	10.00				10.00					
			167.58	20.47	0.00	73.87	15.10	16.76	0.00	12.10	21.28	8.00

- The totals of the VAT columns for the month is the input VAT which can be claimed on the relevant quarter's VAT return.

> For XYZ Designs the total VAT for the three months is £3.25 + £3.64 + £20.47 = £27.36

Further points to note

- If employees' expense claims are settled by cheque, analyse the claim in the petty cash book and enter the cheque in the payments cash book in the column called 'petty cash'. The VAT should be analysed in the petty cash book.

- All cheques drawn for petty cash could be listed on the left hand side of the petty cash book if a proper petty cash tin is maintained.

- You should not worry about a 'balance' of petty cash unless you maintain a separate tin with a float. If you do this you will need to keep two separate petty cash books. One will show expenses paid out of your own pocket, personal cheques and credit cards, and the other will show cash payments made with cash from the tin only. That book will also need to show all money which you put into the tin. The balance for that petty cash book at any time should equal the balance in the petty cash tin. Few artists would find any benefit in operating such a system.

Checklist

This will help guide you as to where each piece of paper should go if you get stuck. Read up on the accounting record mentioned to clarify exactly how the entry should be made and cross refer to the example pages.

You raise a sales invoice

- Write it in the sales day book.
- File it in an unpaid sales invoices file.

You receive payment for a sales invoice

- Mark the invoice paid in the sales day book.
- Write the paying-in-book details in the cash receipts book.
- Refer to the sales invoice or the sales day book in order to analyse out the VAT on the sales invoice in the cash receipts book.

- File the paid invoice in reference number order in the paid sales invoices file.

You receive an invoice from a supplier which you will pay for by a business cheque

- File it in the unpaid invoices file.

You pay a supplier's invoice by a business cheque

- Write the cheque details in the payments cash book.
- Analyse out the VAT from the supplier's invoice in the payments cash book.
- Give the invoice a consecutive reference number and file it in the paid invoices file in number order.

You pay for an item by cash

- Write the details in the petty cash book, analysing out VAT if appropriate.
- Give the receipt or voucher a reference number.
- File the receipt or voucher in a separate petty cash payments file.

You pay for a business item by cheque from your personal bank account and you also have a business bank account

- Follow the previous point and treat it the same as petty cash.

You pay for a business item by a business or personal credit card

- Follow 'how you pay by cash' above exactly.

You receive a statement from a supplier

- Refer to unpaid invoices in your unpaid invoices file to ensure that the supplier's statement is correct. Tick off the supplier's statement when you make payment of the outstanding invoices. You may then file the supplier's statement with the paid invoices in the paid invoices file if you wish. You need do nothing else with it except use the remittance advice to make payment if necessary.

You send a statement to a customer

- File it in a separate file or at the back of your sales invoices.
- Do not make any entry in your books.

You receive a credit note from a supplier

- If you receive a credit note before making payment you should file it in the unpaid invoices file with the appropriate invoice. When you make payment of the net amount you should ensure that the VAT shown in the VAT column of the analysed payments cash book is the net amount of the VAT shown on the original purchase invoice, less the VAT shown on the accompanying credit note.

You receive a credit note from a supplier after you have made payment

- If this is not a major supplier with whom you do continuing business, you should receive a refund from the supplier. The best way to write this out is to show this as a negative payment in your analysed payments cash book, analysing out the VAT from the credit note, giving the credit note a reference in line with the reference numbers given to supplier invoices and filing the credit note in the paid invoices file in sequence with the paid invoices. You should write the credit note details in red and put brackets around the figures to ensure that the credit note shows as a negative amount in the payments cash book.

- If the supplier is a continuing supplier and you have already made payment, the supplier may expect you to net the credit note against the next purchase invoice which you pay. In this case the credit note should be attached to the next purchase invoice which you pay and, as for the point above, only the net VAT amount of the original purchase invoice less the subsequent credit note should be entered in the payments cash book.

You raise a credit note to a customer

- Enter it in the sales day book but mark it as a credit note and write it in brackets or red ink.
- Staple the credit note to a copy of the invoice to which it relates and give it the same reference if possible.
- When you receive payment of the original invoice less your credit note, show the net VAT amount in the VAT column of the receipts cash book.

You receive a delivery note or an order form from a supplier

- Staple it and file it with the invoice when it arrives.
- Do not make any entry in your books.

You receive your bank statement

- Enter the non-cheque payments in the payments cash book.
- Check that there is nothing unusual on the statement.
- Tick off all the cheques from your payments cash book to it and all the receipts from your receipts cash book against it.

You pay an employee's expense claim

- Analyse the expenses in the petty cash book.
- Write the amount of the cheque in the payments cash book in a 'petty cash' column.
- Analyse the VAT in the petty cash book and file supporting vouchers for the claim with petty cash vouchers.

You pay an employee

- It is outside the scope of this book to discuss PAYE in detail. You should however have a PAYE scheme. Talk to your accountant about this. This is referred to in more detail in the chapter on 'Artist as employer'.
- Enter the net pay in the payments cash book in a column called 'wages'.

You pay the employees' tax

- Enter the amount paid in the payments cash book in a column called 'Inland Revenue'.

You pay Customs & Excise your VAT

- Enter the amount paid in an analysis column in the payments cash book called 'Customs & Excise'.
- Do not enter the payment in the VAT column of the payments cash book.

You pay yourself

- Enter the amount in a column in the payments cash book called 'drawings'.

You pay your own tax to the Inland Revenue

- Enter the amount paid in a column in the payments cash book called 'Inland Revenue'. This should be annotated with a description that it is your own tax and not employees' PAYE.

You pay something and do not know where to enter it

- Enter the amount in a column in the payments book called 'sundries' with a full description.

Easier bookkeeping

- Always write a full description, including invoice numbers and discount taken if any, the date and the amount paid on all your cheque book stubs.
- Always write who you received money from on your paying-in-book slip, including the bank's copy.
- File all unpaid suppliers' invoices in one file. When you pay the invoice give it a reference number and file it in order in the paid invoices file. Mark the invoice 'paid' and write on it the cheque number of the cheque used to pay it.
- File or keep all sales invoices in reference number order. You might like to keep all unpaid sales invoices in a separate file.
- File your petty cash receipts in reference number order, by stapling or sticking the vouchers to A4 paper and filing.
- Retain all your records in order in a safe place. For VAT purposes your records must be retained for a minimum of six years.

Double-entry bookkeeping

The bookkeeping system described in this chapter is not a full double-entry bookkeeping system. If you require a double-entry system, the system described in this chapter would need to be expanded to include a purchase day book, a purchase and sales ledger and a nominal ledger. Such systems are normally required for larger businesses, or where there is a requirement for regular management accounts information. In such circumstances, a computerised system is most likely to be appropriate. There are a large number of computerised accounting packages on the market and you should get advice from your accountant or another specialist to find a package which suits your business.

Specimen VAT Return Form

VAT return

To prepare a VAT return, figures must be entered calculated as follows:

Box 1

- Take the monthly total figures for the three months in the quarter from the 'VAT memorandum' columns in the cash receipts book and add these up.

In XYZ Designs, it is £1303.75 plus £647.50 plus £1316.88 making a total of £3268.13.

Box 2

- This refers to purchases from the EU. There are detailed rules concerning the VAT treatment of purchases from other EU member states. Whether or not these are relevant to you will depend on the type of goods or services bought. The detailed rules are outside the scope of this book, and if you trade within the EU you should seek detailed advice from your accountant or Customs & Excise.

131

Box 3

• This is the total of boxes 1 and 2.

Box 4

• Take the monthly total figures for the three months in the quarter from the VAT columns in the analysed cash payments book and add these up. Then add on the totals of the VAT columns for the same months from the petty cash book.

• Make sure you are not claiming for any items which should have been disallowed (that is entertaining, non-business items, items with no VAT receipt, etc).

> In XYZ Designs you would add up £526.48 plus £385.79 plus £365.19 plus £3.25 plus £3.64 plus £20.47 making a total of £1304.82.

Box 5

• This is Box 3 less Box 4.

Box 6

• This is the net value of your sales cash received taken from the receipts cash book. To get this figure you should always take the totals of the 'sales' column in the receipts cash book and minus from this the total of the 'VAT memorandum' column in the receipts cash book.

> For XYZ Designs the total of the 'sales' column for the quarter is £8753.75 plus £4347.50 plus £8841.88 which equals £21,943.13 in total. The total of the 'VAT memorandum' column for the quarter is £3268.13 as previously calculated for Box 1. Therefore £21,943.13 less £3268.13 is £18,675.00 which is the net value of sales in the quarter which goes in Box 6. In most cases to check that your return is so far correct take 17.5% of Box 6 and check that it equals the VAT in Box 1. In XYZ Designs 17.5% x £18,675.00 = £3268.13. If you have had zero-rated or exempt supplies then this will of course not work.

Box 7

• To arrive at the figure for this box add up all the analysis columns in the payments cash book for the months concerned. To this figure add the totals of the petty cash book analysis columns for the same months. From this figure you should then deduct the net amount of wages payments, PAYE and NIC payments, money put into or drawn out of the business, loans, grants or gifts of money, and compensation payments and insurance claims. The resulting figure should then be entered in the box.

For XYZ Designs all analysis columns in the analysed cash payments book for the quarter should be added except for the drawings column. This equals £7299.73. For the petty cash book all the analysis columns should be added. This equals £322.91. Therefore the total in Box 7 is £7299.73 plus £322.91 which equals £7622.64. This figure is rounded to the nearest pound to enter in Box 7.

Box 8 and 9

- These relate to the total sales and purchases to countries within the EU. As stated for Box 2 above, the detailed rules relating to the EU are outside the scope of this book, and if you trade with the EU you should seek detailed advice from your accountant or Customs & Excise.

Declaration

- Print your name.
- Sign and date the form.

Send the form to Customs & Excise in the envelope they supply with the return. Make sure it reaches them by the last day of the month following the end of the period to which the return relates to avoid a penalty.

Petrol

There are regulations regarding VAT and petrol, where petrol is also used for private motoring. If you claim back VAT on petrol, then in Box 1 you must add a scale charge as set out by Customs & Excise. The scale charge varies according to the cc of the car and whether it is a petrol or diesel engine. In tax year 1995/6, for a 1401 – 2000 cc petrol engine, the quarterly VAT to be included in box 1 is £30.09 and the scale charge to be entered in Box 6 is £202. The scale charge figures normally change annually.

If you want to avoid this scale charge then either you must claim back no VAT on the petrol or you must claim back only the petrol on your business mileage and keep an accurate and detailed log of all miles driven to prove this is what you have done.

20 • Ceasing to trade

If you decide you no longer wish to trade as an artist, either because you are retiring, or you simply want to stop, then you should make sure you notify everyone that you are no longer in business. This means current customers (although it might be worth leaving them until after they have paid you) and your suppliers, and you should make settlement of all money outstanding to them, your bank, your landlord if you rent a studio, the Inland Revenue, and Customs & Excise if you are VAT registered. It is important to notify everybody on a prompt basis.

If you are a partnership and one partner leaves the other carrying on the business, then it is worth not only notifying all your customers, suppliers, bank, as well as the Inland Revenue and Customs & Excise, but also putting an advertisement in the local paper or a national publication called the *London Gazette,* notifying the world in general that there is no longer a partnership. It is important that if you are the partner leaving, your name is removed from the headed paper to avoid you continuing to be liable for partnership debts.

If you are a director leaving a limited company you should make sure that you sign a form *G288* notifying the Registrar of Companies that you are no longer a director.

Cessation

When you cease to be self-employed then your tax liability is worked out up until the date of cessation. The following examples illustrate this.

An artist who has been self-employed for a number of years and has profits for the years 1998/9, 1999/2000, 2000/1 as shown below. They prepare accounts to 5 April and cease to be self-employed on 31 December 2001.

Tax Year	Accounts Year	Period Taxed	Months Taxed	£
1998/99	6 Apr 98 – 5 April 99	6 April 98 – 5 Apr 99	12 months	10,000
1999/00	6 Apr 99 – 5 April 00	6 April 99 – 5 Apr 00	12 months	6000
2000/01	6 Apr 00 – 5 April 01	6 April 00 – 5 Apr 01	12 months	5000
2001/02	6 Apr 01 – 31 Dec 01	6 April 01 – 31 Dec 01	8 months, 25 days	3000

The tax calculations cease when the self-employment ceases. This tax year is the only one where the calculations change and there will be no changes to any other tax year. If there are any overlap profits then these will be deducted from the final taxable profits. With a 5 April year end these will be usually be very low.

If a designer has a year end of 30 April but the same profits and date of cessation as the artist above, then this tax calculations would be as follows:

Tax Year	Accounts Year	Period Taxed	Months Taxed	£
1999/00	1 May 98 – 30 Apr 99	1 May 98 – 30 Apr 99	12 months	10,000
2000/01	1 May 99 – 30 Apr 00	1 May 99 – 30 Apr 00	12 months	6000
2001/02	1 May 00 – 31 Dec 01	1 May 00 – 31 Dec 01	20 months	8000

This demonstrates that with a year end other than 5 April, there are likely to be more than 12 months' profit taxed in the year of cessation. see pages 19-33 'Overlap' profits (see chapter 3 • Tax and self-employment) can be deducted to reduce your tax bill.

If the designer in the above example had an overlap profit, calculated when they where first self-employed, of £1000, this would be deducted from the profit in the year 2001/2 and they would pay tax on a profit of £7000. The current year system is designed to ensure that over the life of your business you pay tax on the full amount of the profits you have made.

Once you have stopped being a self-employed artist, it is quite likely that, if you have no other self-employment or other complications with your tax affairs, you may not in the future be sent a tax return. But if you stop during the course of a tax year, you will probably be asked to complete a tax return for that year. Once all the final assessments have been raised by the Inland Revenue or made by yourself, and you have completed your final tax returns and VAT returns, then your self-employment will have effectively ceased.

Once you have told the Inland Revenue that you have ceased trading, it is quite likely they would want to know what you are doing instead, and details should be provided to them.

With regard to National Insurance, as soon as you decide that you are going to stop being self-employed you should notify the DSS as well as notifying your bank to stop the Class 2 National Insurance contributions.

21 • Further information

Tax enquiry offices

by Sharon McKee Tax enquiry offices are the human side of the Inland Revenue, being the only place where you can have a face-to-face discussion with a trained revenue officer. They can provide general information on all tax matters, help with form-filling or advice on a specific problem. If necessary they will act as a 'liaison office', taking notes during any discussions and then sending them on to the tax office concerned. There is an enquiry office in every major city and they have a complete set of all Inland Revenue leaflets and forms. To find your nearest enquiry office look in the telephone book under 'Inland Revenue' or ask your own tax office.

Business advice

There is a network of Training Enterprise Councils (TECs) across England and Wales, Local Enterprise Councils (LECs) across Scotland and Local Enterprise Development Units across Northern Ireland. These all offer advice and information, run training courses on subjects such as bookkeeping, VAT and taxation, or are contact points for other enterprise agencies or small business advice centres in your area.. To contact them look in the phone book or contact your library as they often have resource centres covering this kind of information.

Courses

Many colleges and other educational centres also offer courses on all aspects of running a small business. To find out what's on offer in your area, ring your local college or ask at the library.

There are also a number of business courses aimed specifically at the arts offering a range of full-time and part-time courses on various aspects of arts administration including financial management.

To find out more about this type of course, ring your local regional arts board. They will also have information about grants which are available to support training. The organisations offering short-courses in the visual arts include:

- **AMTIS (Arts Management Training Initiative Scotland)**, Moray house Institute, Chessel's Land, Holyrood Road, Edinburgh EH8 8AQ, tel 0131 558 6506.
- **Arts Management Centre**, 65 Westgate Road, Newcastle upon Tyne NE1 1SG, tel 0191 221 0419, fax 0191 261 7002.
- **Arts Training Programme**, School of Performing Arts, De Montfort University, Scraptoft Campus, Leicester, LE1 9BH, tel: 0116 257 7804.
- **Arts Training South**, CCE, University of Sussex, Falmer, Brighton, BN1 9QH, tel: 01273 606755.
- **Arts Training South West**, Melville House, 12 Middle Street, Taunton, Somerset TA1 1SH, tel: 01823 334767, fax: 01823 334768.
- **Centre for Arts Management**, Institute of Public Administration & Management, University of Liverpool, PO Box 147, Liverpool, L69 3BX, tel: 0151 794 2916.
- **Interchange Training**, Interchange Studios, Dalby Street, London, NW5 3NQ, tel: 0171 267 5220, contact: 0171 482 5292.
- **NACVS (National Association of Councils for Voluntary Service)**, 3rd Floor, Arundel Court, 177 Arundel Gate, Sheffield, SI2 NU, tel 01742 786636.

Banks

Many high street banks now have small business advisors in some of their larger branches and, while many of them are geared up to providing help for starting a business, they will provide advice on banking and on presenting financial information which can be helpful if you have to prepare a business plan, often a prerequisite for large grant aid. The amount of help you recieve often depends on the advisor you see, and so if you are not happy with the results, ask to see another or try a different bank. They will usually only help if you have an account with that bank, but sometimes the suggestion that you are considering moving your account will get you an initial appointment.

CAB

The Citizens' Advice Bureaux (CAB) provides information and advice on a wide range of subjects, and although they do not specialise in providing financial information or help to businesses, they are still worth contacting as they can help self-employed people. If they themselves cannot deal with a problem, they will be able to suggest another source of help. Common problems they deal with include debt and debt recovery, business rate council tax disputes, and contractual problems with suppliers. There is a CAB in every town in the UK and they can be found through the phone book or your local library.

Contacting accountants

There is no single professional body for accountants. The following are all examining, regulatory and disciplinary bodies and membership is only open to accountants who have passed professional examinations. They are all subject to professional regulations (eg they carry professional indemnity insurance etc). If you have a complaint about a chartered accountant you can write to these bodies, who will consider it and pass it on to the disciplinary body, who will then take appropriate action. There are three seperate Institutes of Chartered Accountants (ICA) in the UK and Eire:

- **ICA (England and Wales)**, PO Box 433, Chartered Accountants Hall, Moorgate Place, London, EC2P 2BJ, tel 0171 920 8100
- **ICA (Scotland)**, 27 Queens Street, Edinburgh, EH2 1LA, tel 0131 225 5673
- **ICA (Ireland)**, 11 Donegall Sqaure South, Belfast, BT1 5JE, tel 01232 321600

Another common body is the Chartered Association of Certified Accountants who can be contacted at 29 Lincolns Inn Fields, London, WC2A 3EE, tel 0171 242 6855.

To find out which association your accountant is a member of, look on their stationery or ask at the initial interview. They should be quite willing to give you the information and explain what the membership means to you as one of their clients.

These bodies all have area offices which hold members' lists. The ICA in England and Wales publishes the *Directory of Firms* each year. This lists all their members by geographical area, including some in Scotland. Most entries have details of firms' specialised interests.

The Crafts Council has a national list of accountants recommended by craftspeople, and regional arts boards often have lists of accountants used by artists in their region. A number of accountants also advertise in *Artists Newsletter.*

22 • Glossary

Asset
Something positive which a business has such as equipment, positive bank balance, debtors etc.

Audit
Inspection of a limited company's books and records by a registered auditor. Companies with a turnover of less than £90,000 a year do not need an audit unless they want one. Companies with a turnover of between £90,000 and £350,000 do not have to be audited but must have a report by an accountant on their accounts.

Bad debt
Person who owes you money and has defaulted for reasons of bankruptcy or dispute and where you know you will never get what you are owed.

Bank loans
Arrangement with a bank where money is advanced to an individual or business to be repaid over an agreed term. Interest is charged.

Base rate
An agreed interest rate which all banks and lending institutions take as a standard interest at a point in time, and to which all their other rates are related.

Capital allowances
Tax allowance given on capital equipment.

Capital expenditure
Expenditure on items of equipment, for example studio furniture or a car. Generally defined as items lasting more than one year and costing more than £50.

Capital gains tax
Tax on the disposal of chargeable property, eg shares, antiques, property other than your domestic residence etc.

Chargeable supply
Sales subject to zero or standard rate VAT.

Company secretary
Officer a limited company must, by law, have who is formally responsible for all statutory matters.

Cooperative
Means by which several persons operate a business taking joint responsibility for work decisions and rewards, usually structured as a limited company.

Credit
Length of time given to a person or business to make payment for goods or services provided.

Cumulative sales
Total of sales made in the past twelve months, calculated to check whether the VAT registration limit has been exceeded, thereby requiring VAT registration within thirty days.

Current year basis
The system of self-employed tax calculation introduced for new business from 6 April 1994, or existing businesses from 6 April 1997, where tax is paid on the profits earned in the tax year.

Customs & Excise
Government body which collects VAT and customs duties.

Default surcharge notice
Notice issued by Customs & Excise to a VAT-registered person who has submitted a VAT return late once in a twelve-month period. If a second late return occurs in the period, the trader will be penalised.

Direct debit
An authority issued to a reputable company or individual to take money from a person's bank account at regular intervals. If any increase in the sum is necessary no new documentation has to be completed.

Direct expenses
Expenses which vary in accordance with how much work you do, and are directly related to the work you do, such as art materials, printing, framing, etc.

Drawings
Amounts taken from an incorporated business by a proprietor or owner.

Income tax return
Form sent to you by the Inland Revenue around 5 April asking for details of all sources of income and outgoings and claims for allowances. Must be returned by 31 October. From 5 April 1997 the return must be submitted by 30 September or 31 January.

Independent financial advisor
A financial consultant usually selling pensions, life assurance, permanent health insurance and other investments who is not linked with any insurance company but who must act in their client's best interests and is regulated to ensure they do so.

Inland Revenue
Government body which collects Income Tax, Corporation Tax, Capital Gains Tax, Inheritance Tax, etc.

Input VAT
VAT on goods and services bought which can be offset against your output VAT.

Insolvent/insolvency
Limited company which has become unable to trade because it cannot meet its liabilities as they fall due. An insolvent company usually goes into liquidation. If this happens, directors can be personally responsible for the company's liabilities.

Interest
Sum of money charged for borrowing money or paying money late, either by a bank or lending institution or the Inland Revenue.

Invoice
Document sent out by a person for services rendered or goods supplied stating details of the goods or services together with the cost.

Joint ventures
One or more persons embarking on a similar business or line of work who agree to share resources but who still wish to have separate businesses.

Lending rate
The rate above the base rate which a bank or lending institution will agree to lend money at.

Liabilities
Amounts of money you owe.

Limited company
Business constituted under the Companies Acts. Any liability of a limited company is limited to the value of the share capital, but in practice most limited companies have to give guarantees from the directors in order to trade.

Liquidation
Administration of an insolvent company by an approved liquidator who tries to ensure that as many of the people who are owed money as possible get paid, even if only partially.

National Insurance
Levy paid to the Department of Social Security to safeguard social security and pension rights

Output VAT
VAT on your sales.

Overdraft
Facility granted by a bank whereby a person may draw more money from the bank than they currently have in the account.

Overhead expenses
Expenses incurred in running your business which do not vary regardless of how much work you do. For instance rent, salaries, subscriptions etc.

Partnership
Person trading together with one or more other persons.

PAYE
Pay As You Earn, the system of deducting tax and National Insurance from employees and paying this over to the government on a cumulative month by month basis.

Personal allowances or personal tax allowances
Each taxpayer has an allowance of £3525 (1995/6) for married couples, single parents, widows and the elderly.

Profit
Difference between your income and expenditure. If this is negative it is called a loss.

Prior year basis
The system of tax where people who were self-employed before 6 April 1994 pay tax, calculated by reference to profits earned in the previous year.

Schedule D
Schedule of the Taxes Act under which self-employed persons are charged income tax.

Self-assessment
New system of tax administration introduced from 5 April 1997 whereby taxpayer-assess their own tax liability and make payment on account rather than the Inland Revenue raising assessments.

Self billing
Document issued by an organisation under a scheme arranged by Customs & Excise whereby a VAT registered individual does not need to send a sales invoice.

Sole trader
Person trading on their own.

Standing orders
Arrangement like a direct debit, but the order only lasts for a fixed period of time. If the price increases, new paperwork must be completed.

Tax assessment
Form issued by the Inland Revenue showing the composition of your tax liability and how it is calculated. There are thirty days to appeal against an incorrect tax assessment. This will change after 5 April 1997 – see 'self-assessment'.

Tax computation
Calculation to submit to the Inland Revenue showing the amount of tax owing for a year of assessment.

Tax deductable expenses
Expenses the Inland Revenue have agreed can be deducted from your income to result in the profit subject to income tax.

Tax liability
Amount of tax that you have to pay in a tax year (to 5 April).

Tax relief
Expenses, outgoings and allowances which can be used to reduce income chargeable to tax.

Terms of trade
Written statement as to the terms on which the supply of goods or services takes place.

Tied agent
Financial advisor selling investment products who only represents one company.

Trading
Business offering goods or services to the public for payment and with a view to making a profit.

Trading status
Whether you trade as an individual, a limited company or a partnership.

Transitional & transitional rules
The special rules applying only to the calculating of tax in 1996/7 for those who were self-employed before 6 April 1994.

Turnover
Annual sales, income, fees and reimbursed expenses all added together.

VAT cash accounting scheme
Scheme where you account for VAT only if you have received money from your customers, and you only offset VAT that you have actually paid to suppliers.

VAT liability
Amount of VAT a registered person has to pay to HM Customs & Excise once a quarter.

VAT return
Form *VAT 100* issued by Customs & Excise once a quarter for completion by a VAT-registered person.

VAT
Tax charge on the sale of certain goods or services, currently charged at 0%, 8% and 17.5%.

Index

Index

writing them up 27, 98-101; overhead expenses 28-30; reimbursed from company to director 10; for a residency 82; tax deductible 27-30; tax relief on denied 12; that can never be claimed 30
exports, and VAT exemption 109, 110-12, 116, 133

F

Family Credit 50, 51, 53; on Enterprise Allowance 52
fares, zero rated for VAT 110
food, zero rated for VAT 110
foreign travel, as expenses 29
freelance workers: keeping accounts 96-104; status 11, 90
fuel, *see* petrol

G

galleries: arrangement to act as agent of the artist 62; commission as allowable expense 28; legal costs 30; 'self-billing' arrangement 62, 71, 144; terms of trade with 70-1; VAT- registered artist and/or gallery 60-2, 71; work at covered by insurance 84
government agencies, working closely together 16
grants: from TEC, and National Insurance 47; as taxable income 36-7; on VAT accounts 133

H

health insurance 85
heater, as capital allowance 32
hire of equipment 30
hire purchase 30, 80, 116
hobby business 6-7
home 34-5, 96; bills as deductible expenses 29, 34; mortgage, business expense 34; property and uniform business rate 35; rent as deductible expense 28, 34; studio in 6; telephone as deductible expense 34; 'use of home as a studio' 28, 35
hotels, as expenses 29
Housing Benefit 51; on Enterprise Allowance 52; when self-employed 53

I

income book 97
income support 50, 51, 52; when self-employed 53
industrial injuries disablement benefit 47
Inland Revenue 13-14, 16, 40-5; appealing against assessment 44; being on time with your accounts 40-1; and business records 102-3; ceasing to trade 134-6; dealing with direct 40; definition of self-employed 6, 90; enquiries from and requests for supporting information 41-2; help and advice from 17, 38, 40, 94, 137; if they make a mistake or may have treated unfairly 42; interest and penalties on unpaid tax 42; investigations by (and accuracy of the tax return) 26; multiple sources of income 43-4; and PAYE office 93; schedule D reference number 40; self-assessment 41, 102-3; tax owed to you 42; *see also* expenses; tax
Institutes of Chartered Accountants (ICA) 17, 86, 139

insurance 83-6; on artwork and equipment 83-4; business risks policy 83; claims, on VAT return 133; domestic 35; employee 35; endowment life assurance policy 85; exempt form VAT 110; Life assurance 84-5, 86; life insurance and credit protection policy 79-80; motor 29, 35, 83; permanent health 85, 86; public and employers' liability 35, 83; using a broker 84; warnings 86; *see also* pensions
insurance brokers 79, 84, 85, 86
Invalidity Benefit 49, 50
invoices, *see* sales invoices
Ireland, ICA 17, 139

J

joint ventures, as trading status 7, 9, 142

L

leasing: as an overhead expense 30; of studio 30
leasing companies 80
LECs (Local Enterprise Councils) 36, 52, 137
legal aid 55
legal costs: can not be claimed 30; as expenses 30
Life assurance 84-5
limited company 142, 143; accounts 16; benefit-in-kind charges 27-8; director leaving 134; director of 7, 8, 10, 11, 27, 114; Enterprise Allowance 52; expenses claims 27-8; National Insurance 10; opening a credit account with a supplier 73; sales invoice 63; shareholders 7, 8, 10, 11; VAT accounting 114; as trading status 7-8, 10-11; VAT (chargeable supplies) 57; and VAT on fuel 112-13; VAT registration 16
liquidation 11, 142, 143
loans 7, 76, 80; interest on 30, 77-8; as investment for Enterprise Allowance 52; on VAT return form 133
local authorities, grants from taxable income 36, 37
London Gazette 134
low income: benefits and legal aid 48, 55; Housing Benefit and Council Tax Benefit 51; Income Support 51; lower earnings limit 55; National Insurance exception 53; unable to afford an accountant and dealing with IR direct 40

M

make-up and costumes, as expenses 30
materials: cost of in pricing work 88-9; expenses 28, 91, 100; as expenses during residency 82; purchase from suppliers 73
Maternity Allowance, when self-employed 53
medical care abroad 55
medical expenses, not claimable 30
mortgages: claiming tax relief on mortgage interest 26; on home 28, 34-5; insurance policies 85; on studio 28, 35; on tax return 25
motor expenses 29, 35-6, 87; car parking, VAT claims 109; dual purpose expenditure on 27, 35-

Index

90; rent or mortgage interest on 28; sub-contractor working in 38; tax relief on expenses for employee 91; wages for staff 28

sub-contracting 93; costs 28; employers' liability insurance 83; payment and PAYE 38

subscriptions, as expenses 30, 91

subsistence if working away from home, as expenses 29

suppliers 73-5; and artist ceasing to trade 134; complaining to 74-5; credit account with 73; credit allowed by (expenses book) 101-2; credit notes from in VAT accounts 128; delivery note or order form from in VAT accounts 128; documentation 73-4; invoices form (VAT accounts) 127, 130; statement from for VAT accounts 73, 127; taking credit from (expenses book) 101; VAT invoices from, checked during VAT control visit 108; VAT receipts from 106

T

tax 5; calculation on 'prior year' and current year basis 20-1; capital allowances (business use percentage) 36; capital expenditure and allowances 31-3, 140; ceasing to trade 21, 22, 23, 134-6; changes in the system 5, 27; computation 31; dates on which to be paid 19-20; dual purpose expenditure 35-6; on Enterprise Allowance 52; how it is worked out 19; if not enough earned 19; liability reduced on pension policy 85; married couple's allowance 44, 45; multiple sources of income 43-4; overlap profits 21-2, 23, 25; overlap relief 23; for a partnership 9; and payments to staff/employees 38; for people 'resident' and 'domiciled' in the UK 39; for people working or selling abroad 39; personal allowances 19, 44-5, 143; refunds 19, 20, 26, 43; relief on 26, 27, 73; and residencies 81-2; revenue expenditure 31; self- assessment system 20, 27, 41, 102-3, 144; and self- employment 19-33; single person's allowance 44, 45; and sponsorship 37; status disputes with 91- 2; supporting information and enquiries from IR 41-2; tax relief on Class 4 NI 46; tax return form 25-7; transitional rules from 'prior year' to 'current year' basis 24-5, 145; VAT fines, no relief on 59; working abroad 39; working at home 34-5; year end accounting 22-4, 25; *see also* expenses

tax enquiry offices 137

tax forms: *P14* 94-5; *P15* 38; *P35* 94-5; *P45* 43; *P46* 38; *P60* (certificate of pay and deductions) 26, 43, 92, 94

teaching: income from 25, 43-4; income and National Insurance 47; tax refund claimed on income 26

TECs 36, 137; and the Enterprise Allowance 52; grant and National Insurance 47

telephone: call from telephone box, and claiming VAT on 109; as expenses 27, 29, 34, 87

television, as capital allowance (business use percentage) 32, 36

terms of trade 63-6

textile workers: capital allowances 36; direct costs allowable 28

tied agent 79, 145

trading status 7-11, 15

travel: costs 29, 87; domestic and business expenditure 35-6; expenses 100; expenses in employment 91; as expenses for residency 82; foreign, as expenses 29; home to work not allowable 30, 35; medical and Social Security abroad 55

U

Unemployment Benefit 47, 49, 50-1; and qualification for Enterprise Allowance 52; when self-employed 53

V

VAT 57-62, 105-13, 145; accounts 144-33; business items 106; and cars and petrol 109, 112-13; cash accounting system 60-2, 108, 114, 115-30; chargeable supplies 57; charging at standard rate 105; charging at the wrong rate 109; checklist, of paperwork 126-9; control visits 108-9; de-registration 60; documentation for all purchases 73; 'drawings' 129, 142; exempt 106, 110-11; and galleries 60-2, 71; input VAT 142; and joint ventures (re-charges) 9; mistakes 112; normal basis of accounting 60, 114; payments cash book 121- 4, 127, 128, 129, 132; petty cash book 124-6, 127, 129, 132, 133; problems with 109; purchase invoice listing 114; receipts 105, 106-7; receipts cash book 118-21, 126, 128, 129, 131, 132; re-charged expenses 9, 115, 118; reclaiming 27, 59, 61, 105-7, 108, 109, 112; registered 105-13; registration for 15-16, 58; and residencies 81, 82; returns 107-8, 109, and excuses for late submission 107-8, and penalties if submitted late 107; sales day book 116-18, 120, 126, 128; sales of exempt items 106; sales invoices 63, 64, 126; specimen return form 131-3; and sponsorship 37; 'sundries 129; voluntary registration 59-60; warning 58-9; when you need to register 57-8; and working abroad 39; zero rated items 37, 105, 109-10, 111

video, as capital allowance (business use percentage) 32, 36

W

Wales: ICA 17, 139; Registrar of Companies 10; TECs 52, 137

washing machines, as capital allowance (business use percentage) 36

water rates, zero rated for VAT 110

Widow's Benefit 49, 50

widow's payment 46

widows' pensions 46

Artists Handbooks

A growing series which reports on key aspects of contemporary visual arts practice. They combine analysis and commentary by visual arts experts with the thoughts and experiences of professional artists. Invaluable not only to artists, makers and photographers at all stages of their careers, art and design students, arts organisers, educationalists, careers and business advisers, but to all involved in promotion and development of the visual arts.

Art with People

Who is art for? Ever since community arts emerged in the '60s, there's been debate around this thorny question. And the arguments about process versus product, popular versus 'high' art and individual versus collective responsibility are as much aired now as they were then. *Art with People* traces the cultural and political aspirations of the early pioneers and sets them beside the environment for artists nowadays. By examining why artists choose to engage directly with people as animateurs, artists in residence and through community projects, the book shows how such working practices make the question "art for whom?" a millennium issue.

Chapters cover historical and contemporary context of community arts, artists' residencies, community initiatives, media-based projects and community education work. Writers include Sally Morgan, Felicity Allen, Esther Salamon, Suhail Khan, Sean Cubitt, and Nicholas Lowe. Artists and Groups featured include Open Hand Studios, Camerawork and Catalyst Arts, Alison Marchant and Ken Wolverton.
Ed. Malcolm Dickson, PB, A5, 136pp, illus, ISBN 0 907730 23 X, £7.25

Artists' Stories

What do visual artists do? Paint pictures, design seats, have families, run galleries, construct bridges, shoot films, make sculpture, get into debt, travel the world. A 'career' can mean doing many different things at the same time, involve radical changes of direction and be interrupted by personal circumstances. Keeping work going may often not be easy or remunerative. In *Artists' Stories* up-and-coming and well-established artists, makers and photographers describe how it's worked out for them. Aimed at art and design students, recent graduates and arts educationalists, this book also deserves to be read by all involved in the development of visual arts.

Features 24 artists including Richard La Trobe-Bateman, Lei Cox, John Darwell, Hilary Green, Jane Hamlyn, Karen Knorr, Mary O'Mahony and Janice Tchalenko, Mike Stubbs.
Anna Douglas, Nick Wegner, PB, A4, 80pp, illus, ISBN 0 9077 24 8, £7.25

Investigating Galleries
the artist's guide to exhibiting

The question of how to get work seen by more than the cat and the gasman is answered in this book. Full of information and strategies to improve an artist's chance of exhibiting and minimise the risk of rejection and discouragement, it explains why artists need to investigate their own self-image, ambitions and long-term aspirations and have a clear understanding of how the art world operates before they embark on an exhibiting career. Sound advice on approaching galleries and presenting work, on sales commission, promotion and gallery education strategies means that artists who are young or isolated will find this book invaluable, and the more experienced will discover it inspires new approaches and a sharper plan of action.
Debbie Duffin, PB, A5, 120pp, illus, ISBN 0 907730 22 1, £7.25

Visual Arts Contracts

Introduction to Contracts

Designed to be read as the first step to making professional legal agreements, *Introduction to Contracts*, outlines the elements and terms you might find in a contract, and provides artists with the ammunition they need to negotiate, deal with disputes and find a suitable solicitor.
PB, A4, 12pp, £1.50

Residencies

Demystifies the legal arrangements for artists' residencies in any kind of settings. The ready-to-use contract form for a residency deals with having more than one partner in an agreement, and the workshop contract can be adapted for many 'one-off' activities. Also contains notes on employment and tax, copyright, moral and reproduction rights.
PB, A4, 20pp, ISBN 0 907730 25 6, £3.50

Commission Contracts

Maps out the legal arrangements necessary for all those who work with commissions and public art. By comparing public and private arrangements and describing the roles of parties in public art commissions, functions of agents and dealers and the implications of sub-contracting. Fill-in contract forms for Commissioned Design, Commission and Sale for Public Art and Private Commission Contract.
PB, A4, 20pp, £3.50

Licensing Reproductions

Make the most of your images by getting the licensing agreements right. This contract sets out how to grant or obtain permission to reproduce artwork or designs, and includes details of what licensing agreements to use, and notes on fees and royalties and negotiating and monitoring agreements.
PB, A4, 20pp, £3.50

NAA Public Exhibition Contract

The National Artists Association, commissioned this contract to cover the legal arrangements surrounding showing work in public galleries and exhibition spaces. Many artists, makers and photographers as well as galleries have found it an invaluable way to clarify responsibilities. It includes ready-to-use contract forms for a public exhibition and an exhibition tour, along with information on fees, selling, insurance and promotion.
PB, A4, 24pp, £3.50

Selling Contracts

If selling is part of your practice, then you need this contract. It deals exclusively with selling art and craft work and covers selling to private buyers, galleries and shops, and includes a contract form for selling on sale or return.
PB, A4, 14pp, £3.50

Ordering details

For mail orders add £1.50 per order for postage (UK), £2.50 per order (Europe), £4 per order (Overseas). Telephone credit card orders to 0191 514 3600 (Ref EI), or write to: AN Publications, PO Box 23, Sunderland SR4 6DG (prices quoted at May '95 are subject to change, please check before ordering).

Developed because the visual arts profession needed effective agreements to cover all aspects of contemporary visual arts practice, our Visual Arts Contracts will ensure that collaborations between artists, exhibition organisers, agents, and commissioners are professional and harmonious. Written by Nicholas Sharp – a solicitor specialising in contract preparation and negotiation for business and the arts – they are legally sound, and contain either ready-to-fill-in forms or a point-by-point checklist with explanatory notes. Each comes with permission for the purchaser to make additional copies for their own professional use.